# THE TOMMY'S HANDBOOK

# THE TOMMY'S HANDBOOK

NEIL R. STOREY

*Cover illustrations*: Front: Diagram illustrating the 'on guard' position. Back: Figure for target practice; Fry's cocoa advertisement. All taken from contemproary manuals.

First published 2014

The History Press
The Mill, Brimscombe Port
Stroud, Gloucestershire, GL5 2QG
www.thehistorypress.co.uk



British Library Cataloguing in Publication Data.
A catalogue record for this book is available from the British Library.

ISBN 978 0 7509 5568 3

Typesetting and origination by The History Press
Printed in Great Britain

# CONTENTS

# INTRODUCTION

By the time war broke out in 1914 there were standard military manuals for just about every aspect of training for the British soldier. *The Tommy's Handbook* is a compilation of chapters from original training manuals and booklets that would have been drawn upon by officers, non-commissioned officers and men to train recruits to become soldiers for active service in the First World War. The origins of these manuals can be traced back to the early military manuals of the late eighteenth and nineteenth centuries for the likes of drill, the various rifles used, field engineering and sanitation. It was also not unusual for individual line infantry regiments to produce their own books of standing orders. But then came the new broom: between 1906 and 1912 Richard Burdon Haldane, the Liberal government's Secretary of State for War, had the duty of implementing the Esher Report's recommendations in what became known as the Haldane Reforms – the most dramatic restructuring and redevelopment the British Army had ever experienced.

The greatest task implemented by Haldane was the complete reorganisation of the home field army and reserve system, which created the Territorial Force from the old volunteer system, and the provision of the British Expeditionary Force (BEF). The notion was that the regular battalions would provide the garrison troops for the empire and form a BEF from 'home' garrisoned troops in the event of a 'war emergency', while it was intended that the Territorial Force should remain at home and defend Britain. In 1907 there were

221 battalions of volunteer infantry in England, Scotland and Wales. The new scheme saw line infantry regiment battalions given sequential numbers – i.e. the regular battalions were the 1st and 2nd, the 3rd became a militia or reserve battalion and the 4th and 5th territorial battalions. The Haldane Reforms were officially introduced on 1 April 1908. There were also eleven much heralded cyclist battalions (eight English, two Scottish and one Welsh) included in the scheme. Although soldiers on bicycles may seem a little comical to modern eyes (even at the time they were occasionally referred to as 'gas pipe cavalry'), the military applications for cyclists were seen as a great advance.

Regular soldiers would have a very active life – sports and games, military training and exercises rounded the soldiers' training. Regular battalions served both home and abroad, garrisoning the empire, much as they had done in the nineteenth century. The army had the benefit of the temperance associations within the military to maintain the good work of keeping soldiers sober. Army education was well established and Christian societies – to keep the faith – had also been established in the later nineteenth century. Indeed, the British soldier in India could live very well. Even 'other ranks' soldiers could take their family out there and afford to have servants. Although there were small campaigns, there had been no major conflict since the Anglo-Boer War (1899–1902).

Most of the new territorial battalions were made up of eight companies, each of which consisted of about four officers and a hundred men. Although a few came from outside the battalion's area, most of them would have been local men and just about all parts of the county were represented. The allocation of men to each company depended largely upon which part of the county they lived or worked in. This suited most recruits, who were more than happy to serve with their relations, friends and acquaintances, and it made the battalion a close-knit society. In fact, amongst all ranks each battalion was riddled with complicated family ties of uncles, nephews, brothers and cousins serving side by side and throughout the various companies. Its rank structure reflected society at the time: the officers were from the local gentry or were the directors of larger local industries; the non-commissioned officers were works foremen and ex-servicemen; the other ranks were comprised of domestic staff, labourers, factory or mill workers, gardeners and estate workers. The year 1913 began with a total Army Reserve of 139,077 and an entire Territorial Force of 314,366, all ranks.

With the new regime came new uniforms and new equipment. The Short Magazine Lee-Enfield rifle was the new weapon for the army in the twentieth century. With its easy bolt action, well-trained soldiers could achieve an impressive rate of rapid fire, and it gave a new confidence to the fighting men. Khaki uniforms had already been fully adopted from 1902 as the standard garb of the British soldier, but the 1903 bandolier and belt equipment had not proved as practical as was hoped, so in 1908 the British Army broke with its tradition of leather equipment and a woven fabric 'webbing' was introduced instead. This kit was far more logical and practical than any of its predecessors. It could be adjusted to fit well, it would be blancoed to waterproof and preserve it, and it contained such useful items as an entrenching tool with separate shaft, a bayonet, a water bottle, and large and small packs to carry all the soldier would need when he was on campaign. Groups of cartridge carrier pouches either side of the chest were able to carry 75 rounds of .303 ammunition - 3 clips of 5 rounds - in each pocket. In every way the British Army was reformed and looked new. But despite all this new kit, there was still no equipment that would actually protect the soldier - shrapnel helmets only began to be issued from late 1915.

The reforms were, however, concerned with the future in every way. The creation of an Officer Training Corps (OTC) in public and grammar schools was intended to provide a seedbed of ready-trained patriotic young men fit to be officers and gentlemen in the reformed British Army. The OTC movement had two divisions, 'Senior' based in the universities and 'Junior' working in schools, both established with the express aim of providing as many officers as possible for the Special Reserve and the new Territorial Force. Every week the boys would be mustered to parade for drill, skill at arm and shooting practice and manoeuvres across the school field and surrounding land. There would also be spring and summer OTC camps with other schools. Haldane's vision matured in 1914, and in the first seven months of the war the OTC provided over 20,000 commissioned officers – many of them joining their regiments straight from school.

In the years immediately before the First World War, the British Army was revolutionised by Haldane's reforms. It had not only been restructured but its training was also reformed, with the production of training manuals and regulations that were to be followed as standard across the army. *Field Service Regulations – Operations 1909* was the first in this new series and had been created with careful consideration by an expert team of experienced and skilful staff officers. *Field Service Regulations – Operations* was the first military manual to lay down how the British Army should conduct itself in action, with such chapters as 'The Fighting Troops and their Characteristics', 'Movements by Land and Sea', 'The Battle' and 'Warfare Against an Uncivilised Enemy'. The manual also stated, in detail, staff responsibilities and procedures as diverse as fighting troops and their characteristics, intercommunication and orders, protection, siege operations and night operations, quarters, camps and bivouacs that would ultimately shape the way the British Army was organised and how it conducted operations during the First World War. *Military Operations* and many other manuals were revised and reprinted as the war progressed – the experience of modern battle provided a steep learning curve. In some cases pamphlets and booklets were created in the theatres of war themselves by field printing units and distributed to the trenches direct.

*The Tommy's Handbook* is compiled with family historians, scholars and re-enactors in mind, and aims to answer many of the questions I have been frequently asked at my lectures over the years. It comprises chapters and texts from a selection of the manuals I have collected over the last thirty years – as such, note that there may be occasional references to other parts of the original texts which are not reproduced here. Nonetheless, I hope it will be a useful 'enquire within' volume to dip into as well as a vivid and authentic overview of how a typical British line infantry soldier or 'Tommy' was trained both at home and in the field during the First World War.

*Neil R. Storey*
*2014*

# 1

# RECRUITMENT

Army Form B. 218M.

G.  R.

# HIS MAJESTY'S ARMY.

10*th November*, 1914.

***This Leaflet is intended to take the place of any issued before this date.***

## WEEKLY RATES OF PAY OF PRIVATE SOLDIERS IN THE REGULAR ARMY AND SPECIAL RESERVE.

| ARMS DRAWING PROFICIENCY PAY. | On Enlistment. | After two years' service. | PERIODS OF SERVICE. For the War only, or With Colours. | With Reserve |
|---|---|---|---|---|
| Household Cavalry ... ... | 12/3 | 14/- to 15/9 | 8 yrs. | 4 yrs. |
| Cavalry of the Line ... ... | 8/2 | 9/11 „ 11/8 | 7 „ | 5 „ |
| Horse Artillery— | | | | |
| Gunner ... ... ... ... | 9/4 | 11/1 „ 12/10 | 6 „ | 6 „ |
| Driver ... ... ... ... | 8/9 | 10/6 „ 12/3 | 6 „ | 6 „ |
| Royal Field Artillery ... ... | 8/5½ | 10/2½ „ 11/11½ | 3 „ | 9 „ |
| Royal Garrison Artillery ... ... | 8/5½ | 10/2½ „ 11/11½ | 8 „ | 4 „ |
| Foot Guards ... ... ... | 7/7 | 9/4 „ 11/1 | 3 „ | 9 „ |
| Infantry of the Line ... ... | 7/- | 8/9 „ 10/6 | 7 „ | 5 „ |

| ARMS DRAWING ENGINEER OR CORPS PAY. | On Enlistment. | On completion of recruit training if qualified for corps duties. | Thereafter according to qualifications. | With Colours. | With Reserve. |
|---|---|---|---|---|---|
| Royal Engineers— | | | | 3 yrs. | 9 yrs. |
| Sapper ... ... ... | 11/8 | 15/2 | 17/6 to 22/2 | 6 „ | 6 „ |
| Pioneer ... ... ... | 8/2 | 11/8 | 11/8 | 6 „ | 6 „ |
| Driver ... ... ... | 8/2 | 10/6 | 10/6 to 11/8 | 2 „ | 10 „ |
| Royal Flying Corps ... ... | Special Rates. | | | 4 „ | 4 „ |
| Army Service Corps— | | | | | |
| Supply Branch, Private ... ... ... | 8/2 | 9/11 | 11/8 „ 16/4 | 3 „ | 9 „ |
| Horse Transport Driver ... ... ... | 8/2 | 9/11 | 11/8 | 2 „ | 10 „ |
| Mechanical Transport Section—Artificer ... | 8/2 | 9/11 | 11/8 to 17/6 | 7 „ | 5 „ |
| Driver ... | 8/2 | 9/11 | 11/8 „ 16/4 | | |
| Royal Army Med. ... ... | 8/2 | 10/6 | 11/8 „ 12/10 | 3 „ | 9 „ |
| Army Ordnance Corps ... | 8/2 | 9/11 | 11/8 „ 16/4 | 6 „ | 6 „ |

Pay increases considerably on promotion.

[No. 1.]

**Your King and Country Need You.**

**A CALL TO ARMS.**

An addition of 100,000 men to his Majesty s Regular Army is immediately necessary in the present grave National Emergency.

Lord Kitchener is confident that this appeal will be at once responded to by all those who have the safety of our Empire at heart.

**TERMS OF SERVICE.**

General Service for a period of 3 years or until the war is concluded.

Age of Enlistment between 19 and 30.

**HOW TO JOIN.**

Full information can be obtained at any Post Office in the Kingdom or at any Military depot.

**GOD SAVE THE KING!**

# 2

# DRILL

### 4. *Recruit training.*

1. The course of recruit training should include :—

i. The development of a soldierly spirit.

ii. Instruction in barrack and camp duties, cleanliness, care of feet, smartness, orders, and such regulations as immediately affect the soldier.

iii, Physical training, under qualified instructors, as laid down in the Manual of Physical Training.

iv. Infantry Training, Chapters II to V inclusive.

v. Marching, march discipline, and running.

vi. Musketry instruction under the following heads :—

(*a*) General description of the rifle and ammunition used.

(*b*) Instruction in care of arms.

(*c*) Elementary instruction in the theory of rifle fire.

(*d*) Aiming and firing.

(*e*) Visual training and judging distance.

vii. Movements at night, and practice in using the ears and eyes at night (Sec. 113).

viii. Guards and outposts.

ix. Rudiments of the duties of a soldier in the field.

x. Use of the entrenching implement and entrenching tools.

(xi) Bayonet fighting.

2. Before being dismissed recruit training every regular recruit will be examined by the depôt or battalion commander and a medical officer, who will determine whether he has

attained the necessary standard of efficiency (*see* paragraph 3) and is physically fit for the duties of a trained soldier.

This examination may take place as soon as it is thought that a batch of recruits has attained the required standard, but never later than six months after enlistment, deducting any periods spent in hospital or under detention.

When once a recruit has been passed as above, he must be considered a trained man with the exception of musketry. A recruit must on no account be passed temporarily and the final stages of the syllabus postponed with a view to taking him for other duties in the meanwhile. The entire course of his recruit training (including Table A, if possible, *see* para. 10) must be continuous.

A special report must be made by the depôt or battalion commander, to the district or brigade commander as the case may be, about any line recruit who, after six months training, is found too weak or too awkward for the duties of a trained soldier.

3. The necessary standard of efficiency before a regular recruit is dismissed recruit training is as follows :—

(*a*) The recruit must be able to turn out correctly in marching order and fit to take his place in the ranks of his company in close and extended order drill.

(*b*) Carry out an ordinary route march in marching order.

(*c*) Have completed his recruit gymnastic training.

(*d*) Be sufficiently instructed in musketry and visual training to commence a recruit's course of musketry immediately after being dismissed recruit training.

(*e*) Be sufficiently trained to take part in night operations.

(*f*) Understand the principles of protection and his duties on guard or outpost.

(*g*) Be able to use the entrenching implement and entrenching tools and understand the method of carrying tools.

(*h*) Be well grounded in bayonet fighting.

4. Recruits will be formed in squads for instructional purposes. The number of men in each squad should be as small as the number of available instructors will allow.

5. Squad instructors will be most carefully selected. They must be intelligent, energetic, smart in their bearing, and thoroughly well trained in the art of instruction. It will usually be advantageous for the instructor to remain with the same squad throughout the period of training and carry out the whole of the instruction except physical training, which will be taught only by fully qualified instructors.

6. The course of instruction should be so arranged as to begin with about 20 hours work per week, gradually increasing to about 28 hours work per week. The daily work should be arranged with as much variety as possible, and must be suited to the aptitude of the individual recruit. Every endeavour must be made to avoid monotony, with its consequent loss of interest.

7. A syllabus for a course of six months' training is given in the Appendix to assist officers charged with the training of recruits in framing their programmes. This syllabus, which is published as a guide only, and need not be rigidly followed, is so arranged as to admit of recruits who show special aptitude being dismissed their recruit training at the end of

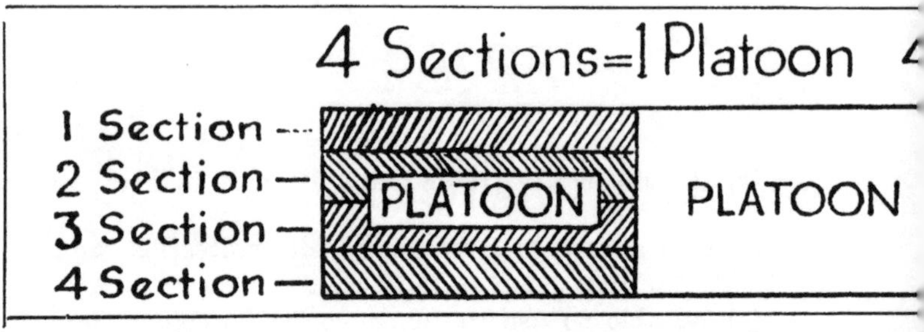

4 Sections=1 Platoon 4

1 Section
2 Section
3 Section
4 Section

PLATOON PLATOON

DIAGRAM SHOWING SECTI

the twentieth week. In addition to the work mentioned in this syllabus recruits must be given practical instruction in laying out kits, the repair of clothing, and the cleaning of clothing and equipment.

8. Equipment will be issued on joining, but, with the exception of waistbelt and cartridge carriers, which will be used for all musketry parades after the first fortnight, it will not be worn on parade during the first month. Instructors will wear waistbelts on all parades, with cartridge carriers on musketry parades.

Dummy cartridges will be used by both instructors and recruits on all musketry parades.

9. Rifles will be issued when the depôt or battalion commander directs, but not earlier than the second week.

10. As soon as possible after being dismissed recruit training young soldiers will be put through Table A. Until this course is begun they will be given five hours a week special musketry instruction.

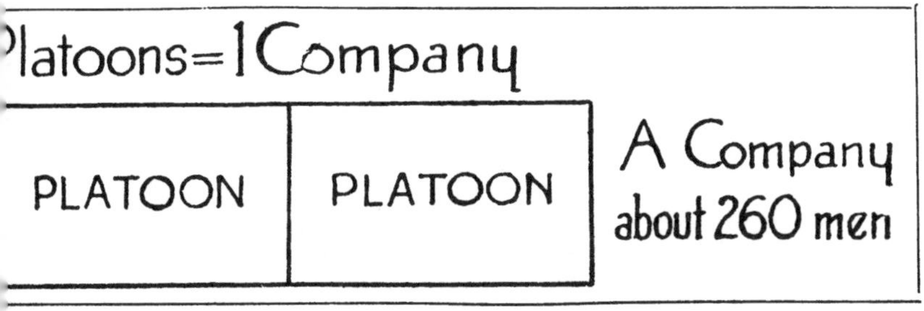

| 'latoons=1 Company | | |
|---|---|---|
| PLATOON | PLATOON | A Company about 260 men |

COMPOSITION OF A COMPANY.

# CHAPTER II.

## SQUAD DRILL.

### 10. *Method of instructing recruits.*

1. The instructor should be clear, firm, concise, and patient; he must make allowance for the different capacities of the men, and avoid discouraging nervous recruits; he must remember that much may be taught by personal example, and that careful individual instruction is the best means of developing the intelligence.

2. The instructor will teach as much as possible by demonstration, performing the movements himself or making a smart recruit perform them. The detail for each movement as given in this manual is for the information of instructors, who must avoid repeating it word for word, because such a method is wearisome and monotonous and would not be understood by some recruits.

The instructor will explain the reason for every movement and formation, and its application in the field.

3. Drills will be short and frequent to avoid the exhaustion of the instructor and recruits.

4. Recruits will be advanced progressively from one exercise to another, men of inferior capacity being put back to a less advanced squad.

5. At first the recruit will be placed in position by the

instructor; afterwards he should not be touched, but made to correct his own position when faults are pointed out.

6. When the various motions have been learnt, instruction "by numbers" will cease.

**11.** *Words of command.*

1. Commands will be pronounced distinctly, and sufficiently loud to be heard by all concerned.

2. Commands which consist of one word will be preceded by a caution. The caution, or cautionary part of a command, will be given deliberately and distinctly; the last or executive part, which, as a rule, should consist of only one word or syllable, will be given sharply: as **Battalion—Halt**; **Right—Form**; **Right hand—Salute**. A pause will be made between the caution and the executive word. Men will be taught to act upon the last sound of the executive word of command.

3. When the formation is moving, executive words will be completed as the men begin the pace which will bring them to the spot on which the command is to be executed. The caution must be commenced accordingly (*see also* Sec. **26**, 1, note).

4. Young officers and non-commissioned officers will be frequently practised in giving words of command.

5. Indistinct and slovenly words of command beget slovenly movements and must be avoided.

6. The cautions and commands in this manual are, as a rule, given with regard to one flank only, but the same principle applies equally to movements to the other flank, which will also be practised.

# SQUAD DRILL WITHOUT ARMS.

## Squad Drill with Intervals.

### **12.** *Formation of squads with intervals.*

1. A few men will be placed in single rank at arm's length apart; while so formed, they will be termed a *squad with intervals.*

2. Instruction can best be imparted to a squad in single rank, but, if want of space makes it necessary, the squad may consist of two ranks, in which case the men of the rear rank will cover the intervals between the men in the front rank, so that in marching they may take their own points, as directed in Sec. **21, 4**.

3. When recruits have learned to dress as described in Sec. **16**, they will be taught to fall in as above described, and then to dress and correct their intervals. After they have been instructed as far as Sec. **26**, they may fall in as directed in Sec. **27**.

4. Recruits formed into a squad will be directed to observe the relative places they hold with each other; while resting between the exercises they may be permitted to fall out and move about; they will be instructed on the command *Fall in,* to fall in as they stood at first.

### **13.** *Attention.**

**Squad—Attention.**

Spring up to the following position :—

Heels together and in line. Feet turned out at an angle

---

* In this and the following sections the title of the section or of the movement is shown in *italics*, and is followed in the next line by the caution or executive word of command in **thick type.** The body of the section contains the detail. Cautions or words of command referred to in the detail are in *italics*.

of about 45 degrees. Knees straight. Body erect and carried evenly over the thighs, with the shoulders (which should be level and square to the front) down and moderately back—this should bring the chest into its natural forward position without any straining or stiffening. Arms hanging easily from the shoulders as straight as the natural bend of the arm, when the muscles are relaxed, will allow, but with the thumbs immediately behind the seams of the trousers. Wrists straight. Palms of the hands turned towards the thighs, hands partially closed, backs of fingers touching the thigh lightly, thumb close to forefinger. Neck erect. Head balanced evenly on the neck, and not poked forward, eyes looking their own height and straight to the front.

The weight of the body should be balanced on both feet, and evenly distributed between the fore part of the feet and the heels.

The breathing must not in any way be restricted, and no part of the body should be either drawn in or pushed out.

The position is one of readiness, but there should be no stiffness or unnatural straining to maintain it.

Particular attention should be paid to the heels being in line, as otherwise the man cannot stand square in the ranks.

### **14.** *Standing at ease.*

**Stand at—Ease.**

Keeping the legs straight, carry the left foot about twelve inches to the left so that the weight of the body rests equally on both feet; at the same time carry the hands behind the back and place the back of one hand in the palm of the other, grasping it lightly with the fingers and thumb, and allowing the arms to hang easily at their full extent. (It is immaterial which hand grasps the other.)

*Notes.*—i. In marching order without the rifle the arms will be retained as in the position of *attention.*

ii. When a recruit falls in for instruction he will *stand at ease* after he has got his dressing.

15. *Standing easy.*

**Stand—Easy.**

The limbs, head, and body may be moved, but the man will not move from the ground on which he is standing, so that on coming to *attention* there will be no loss of dressing. Slouching attitudes are not permitted.

16. *Dressing a squad with intervals.*

**Right—Dress.**

Each recruit, except the right-hand man, will turn his head and eyes to the right and will then extend his right arm, back of the hand upwards, finger tips touching the shoulder of the man on his right. At the same time he will take up his dressing in line by moving, with short quick steps, till he is just able to distinguish the lower part of the face of the second man beyond him. Care must be taken to carry the body backward or forward with the feet, the shoulders being kept perfectly square in their original position.

**Eyes—Front.**

The head and eyes will be turned smartly to the front. the arm dropped, and the position of *attention* resumed.

17. *Turning by numbers.*

**1. Turning to the Right—One.**

Keeping both knees straight and the body erect, turn to

the right on the right heel and left toe, raising the left heel and right toe in doing so.

On the completion of this preliminary movement, the right foot must be flat on the ground and the left heel raised; both knees straight, and the weight of the body, which must be erect, on the right foot.

**Two.**

Bring the left heel smartly up to the right without stamping the foot on the ground.

**2. Turning to the Left—One.**

Turn to the left, as described above, on the left heel and right toe, the weight of the body being on the left foot on the completion of the movement.

**Two.**

Bring the right heel smartly up to the left without stamping the foot on the ground.

**3. Turning About—One.**

Keeping both knees straight and the body erect, turn to the right-about on the right heel and left toe, raising the left heel and right toe in doing so.

On the completion of this preliminary movement, the right foot must be flat on the ground and the left heel raised; both knees straight, and the weight of the body, which must be erect, on the right foot.

**Two.**

Bring the left heel smartly up to the right without stamping the foot on the ground.

# PLATE I.

**4. Inclining to the Right—One.**

As described for turning to the right, but turning only half right.

**Two.**

As described for turning to the right.

**5. Inclining to the Left—One.**

As described for turning to the left, but turning only half left.

**Two.**

As described for turning to the left.

*Note.*—In turning "judging the time" commands are *Right* (or *left* or *about*) *Turn, Right* (or *left*) *Incline* ; the movements described above will be carried out on the word *Turn* or *Incline*, observing the two distinct motions.

**18.** *Saluting to the front.*

1. *By numbers.*

**Salute by Numbers—One.**

Bring the right hand smartly, with a circular motion, to the head, palm to the front, fingers extended and close together, point of the forefinger 1 inch above the right eye, or touching edge of peak of cap just above right eyebrow as in illustration, thumb close to the forefinger ; elbow in line, and nearly square, with the shoulder (*see* Plate I).

**Two.**

Cut away the arm smartly to the side.

## 2. SQUAD DRILL WITH ARMS.

### Rifle Exercises.

#### **47.** *General rules.*

1. Recruits, before they commence the rifle exercises, are to be taught the names of the different parts of the rifle and the care of arms.

2. The rifle exercises will not be performed at inspections, and will only be practised by units larger than a squad for purposes of ceremonial.

3. Instruction in the rifle exercises should be combined with aiming and firing instruction.

Squad drill with arms should be practised occasionally in extended order (*see* Chap. V) to accustom recruits to handle their arms steadily and correctly when separated from their comrades.

4. The following instructions apply to the short Lee-Enfield, Lee-Enfield, and Lee-Metford rifle. A special note is made when the instructions for the short Lee-Enfield rifle do not apply to the Lee-Enfield or Lee-Metford rifle.

5. The recruit having been thoroughly instructed in the rifle exercises by numbers, will be taught to perform them in quick time, the words of command being given without the numbers, and executed as detailed in the following sections, with a pause of one beat of quick time between each motion.

6. Squads drilling with rifles will be practised in the different marches and variations of step described in the foregoing sections.

The disengaged arm will be allowed to swing naturally as described in Secs. **21** and **24**.

**48.** *Falling in with arms at the order* (Plate V).

The recruit will fall in as described in Sec. **27**, with the rifle held perpendicularly at his right side, the butt on the ground, its toe in line with the toe of the right foot. The right arm to be slightly bent, the hand to hold the rifle at or near the band (with the Lee-Enfield or Lee-Metford rifle, near the lower band), back of the hand to the right, thumb against the thigh, fingers together and slanting towards the ground.

When each man has got his dressing he will *stand at ease.*

**49.** *To stand at ease from the order.*

**Stand at—Ease.**

Keeping the legs straight, carry the left foot about 12 inches to the left so that the weight of the body rests equally on both feet. At the same time incline the muzzle of the rifle slightly to the front with the right hand, arm close to the side, the left arm to be kept in the position of *attention.*

*Note.*—The procedure is the same with or without bayonets fixed.

**50.** *The attention from stand at ease.*

**Squad—Attention.**

The left foot will be brought up to the right and the rifle returned to the *order.*

**51.** *The slope from the order.*

**Slope Arms—One.**

Give the rifle a cant upwards with the right hand, catching it with the left hand at the back-sight and the right hand

## PLATE V.

at the small of the butt, thumb to the left, elbow to the rear.

**Two.** (Plate VI.)

Carry the rifle across the body, and place it flat on the left shoulder, magazine outwards from the body. Seize the butt with the left hand, the first two joints of the fingers grasping the upper side of the butt, the thumb about one inch above the toe, the upper part of the left arm close to the side, the lower part horizontal, and the heel of the butt in line with the centre of the left thigh.

**Three.**

Cut away the right hand to the side.

**52.** *The order from the slope.*

**Order Arms—One.**

Bring the rifle down to the full extent of the left arm, at the same time meeting it with the right hand between the back sight and the band (at the lower band, Lee-Enfield and Lee-Metford rifle), arm close to the body.

**Two.**

Bring the rifle to the right side, seizing it at the same time with the left hand round the nose cap (at the upper band, Lee-Enfield and Lee-Metford rifle), butt just clear of the ground.

**Three.**

Place the butt quietly on the ground, cutting the left hand away to the side.

# 3

# RIFLES, BAYONETS & GRENADES

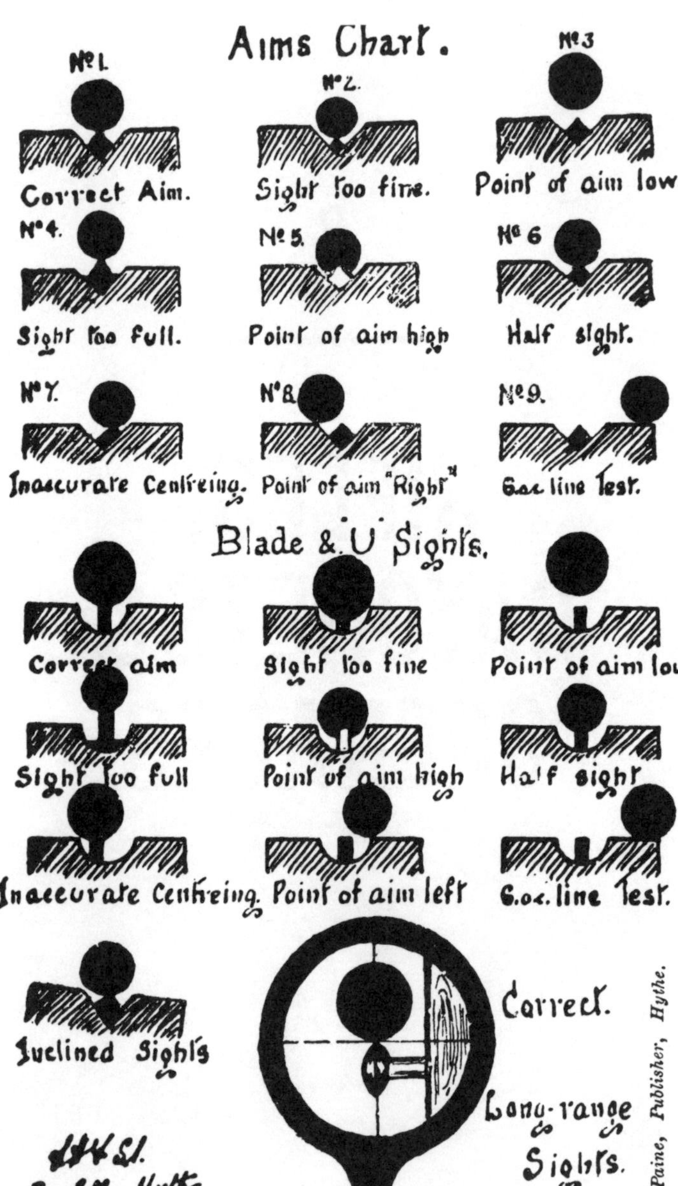
Aims Chart.
No 1.
No 2.
No 3
Correct Aim.
Sight too fine.
Point of aim low.
No 4.
No 5.
No 6
Sight too full.
Point of aim high
Half sight.
No 7.
No 8
No 9.
Inaccurate Centreing.
Point of aim "Right"
S.o.c. line Test.
Blade & U Sights.
Correct aim
Sight too fine
Point of aim low
Sight too full
Point of aim high
Half sight
Inaccurate Centreing.
Point of aim left
S.o.c. line Test.
Inclined Sights
Correct.
Long-range Sights.
S. of M. Hythe.
Paine, Publisher, Hythe.

## SECTION 3.

### Preliminary Bayonet Lessons.

**16.** Open ranks for bayonet practice as follows:—"Rear Rank—About turn"; "Odd numbers of the front rank and even numbers of the rear rank—Six (or more) paces forward—March," "About turn"; "The whole, one pace right close—March." Or, "For Bayonet practice open—out." **Class arrangements.**

Small classes should be opened out from single rank.

Classes should always work with bayonets fixed.

When teaching a new position, face the class to a flank and let them "rest." First show them the position, explaining essential points and giving the reasons for them. Then show the position a second time, making the class observe each movement, so that, from the very commencement of the bayonet training, a man is taught to use his eyes and brain. Face the ranks and order them to assume the position explained and shown. Pick out the man who shows the best position and let the class look at and copy him. Remember that his position may not be ideal, but it is more correct than those assumed by the remainder, who, being beginners, cannot distinguish the difference between a good position and an ideal one. Many instructors err by trying to get a class of beginners to idealise at once.

**17.** The Recruit's Course consists of five lessons and the Final Assault Practice. The hours in the syllabus for bayonet training are so divided as to give daily practice. The training should be carried out chiefly in a "free and easy" kit, but men should be accustomed to use their bayonets when wearing belt and pouches, and packs may be worn when an efficiency test is in progress. For the **Recruit's Course.**

"pointing" and "parrying" practices a light stick, 5 feet to 5 feet 9 inches long and $1\frac{3}{4}$ inches to 3 inches in circumference, with thrusting ring and pad, must be provided for every two men.

Daily Practice.

18. Half-an-hour a day, on at least five days a week, should be devoted to the daily practice in bayonet fighting by trained soldiers. By this daily practice accuracy of direction, quickness, and strength are developed, and a soldier is accustomed to using the bayonet under conditions which approximate to actual fighting. This half-hour should be apportioned to (1) Pointing at the body; (2) Pointing at thrusting rings, &c., on light sticks at varying distances and directions; (3) Parrying light sticks; (4) Dummy work; and (5), when sufficiently proficient, the Final Assault Practice.

LESSON 1.

"On Guard."

19. Point of the bayonet directed at the base of the opponent's throat, the rifle held easily and naturally with both hands, the barrel inclined slightly (about 30°) to the left, the right hand, over the navel, grasping the small of the butt, the left hand holding the rifle at the most convenient position in front of the backsight so that the left arm is only slightly bent, *i.e.*, the upper arm and fore-arm making an angle of about 150°. The legs well separated in a natural position, such as a man walking might adopt on meeting with resistance, *i.e.*, left knee slightly bent, right foot flat on the ground with toe inclined to the right front.

The position should not be constrained in any way but be one of aggression, alertness, and readiness to go forward for immediate attack (*vide* Plate I).

The "On guard" position will also be taught with the right foot in front.

*Common Faults.*

(1) Leaning body back.
(2) Left arm too much bent.
(3) Right hand held too low and too far back.
(4) Rifle grasped too rigidly, restraining all freedom of movement.

Assume a position of "rest" in the easiest way without moving the feet. "Rest."

The hands holding the rifle as when on guard; the left wrist level with, and directly in front of, the left shoulder; right hand level with and to the right of the buckle of the waist-belt. "High port."

When jumping ditches, surmounting obstacles, &c., the position of the rifle should be approximately maintained with the left hand alone, leaving the right hand free.

**20.** Grasping the rifle firmly, vigorously deliver the point from the "on guard" position to the full extent of the left arm, butt running alongside and kept close to the right forearm. Body inclined forward; left knee well bent; right leg braced, and weight of the body pressed well forward with the fore part of the right foot, heel raised. "Long Point."

The chief power in a "point" is derived from the right arm with the weight of the body behind it, the left arm being used more to direct the point of the bayonet. The eyes must be fixed on the object at which the point is directed. In making "points" other than straight to the front, the left foot should move laterally in the same direction as that in which the "point" is made.

During the later stages of this lesson the men should be practised in stepping forward with the rear foot when delivering the "point."

## SECTION 4.

### Tactical Application of the Bayonet.

**37.** A bayonet assault should preferably be made under cover of fire, surprise, or darkness. In these circumstances the prospect of success is greatest, for a bayonet is useless at any range except hand-to-hand. **Practical use of the bayonet.**

**38.** At night all these forms of cover can be utilised. On the other hand, confusion is inherent in fighting by night; consequently, the execution of a successful night attack with the bayonet requires considerable and lengthy training. Units should be frequently practised in night work with the bayonet. **Night work.**

**39.** The bayonet is essentially a weapon of offence which must be used with skill and vigour; otherwise it has but little effect. To await passively an opportunity of using the bayonet entails defeat, since an approaching enemy will merely stand out of bayonet range and shoot down the defenders. **Bayonet an offensive weapon.**

**40.** In an assault the enemy should be killed with the bayonet. Firing should be avoided, for in the mix-up a bullet, after passing through an opponent's body, may kill a friend who happens to be in the line of fire. **No firing during an assault.**

### Final Assault Practice.

**41. This practice is only to be carried out after the men have been thoroughly trained in all the preliminary lessons, and have acquired complete control of their weapons, otherwise injury to rifles and bayonets will result from improper application of the methods laid down in the foregoing instruction.**

The Final Assault Practice must approximate as nearly as possible to the conditions of actual fighting.

Nervous tension due to the anticipation of an attack, reacting on the body, as well as the advance across the open and the final dash at the enemy, combine to tire an assaulting party. It is only by their physical fitness and superior skill in the use of the bayonet that they can overcome a comparatively fresh foe.

Therefore quick aim and good direction of the bayonet, when moving rapidly or even when surmounting obstacles, accurate delivery of a point of sufficient strength and vigour to penetrate clothing and equipment, clean withdrawal of the bayonet—which requires no small effort, especially should it be fixed by a bone—are of the greatest importance, and need the same careful attention and constant practice as are devoted to obtaining efficiency with the rifle.

In the Final Assault Practice the charge brings the men to the first trench in a comparatively exhausted condition, and the accuracy of the aim is tested by the disc, which can only be "carried" by a true and vigorous thrust and a clean withdrawal.

For this practice the men should be made to begin the assault from a trench six or seven feet deep, as well as from the open, and they should not cheer until close up to the "enemy."

**Final Assault Practice Course.**

**42.** A reproduction of a labyrinth of trenches, with dummies in the "dug-outs" and shelters between the trenches, forms an excellent Final Assault Practice Course. Assaults should be made from all four sides in order to give variety. The edges of the trenches should be protected by spars or baulks anchored back ; otherwise constant use will soon wear them out. Cinders scattered over the course prevent the men from slipping. If gallows cannot be erected, sack dummies should be placed on tripods or on end, as well as lying in trenches or on the parapets, with soft earth free from stones under them.

Commanding Officers will be responsible for the construction of the Final Assault Practice Courses, and will decide on the number, length, and nature of the trenches in accordance with the ground available. Officers in charge of Physical and Bayonet Training, or where there are no such officers Army Gymnastic Staff and Assistant Instructors, will be responsible to Commanding Officers for the upkeep of the courses.

**Tactical schemes.**

**43.** Extremely interesting and practical schemes in trench warfare can be arranged by combining the Final Assault Practice with other branches of training, *e.g.*, bombing, laying sandbags, entrenching.

**Competitions.**

**44.** Competitions can be arranged by allotting or deducting marks for (1) number of discs transfixed and carried on a bayonet, (2) time taken from giving the signal to charge until the last man of the team passes the finishing post, and (3) style.

Competitions should never be carried out until the men have completed their lessons in bayonet training and thoroughly mastered the handling of the bayonet in the Final Assault Practice.

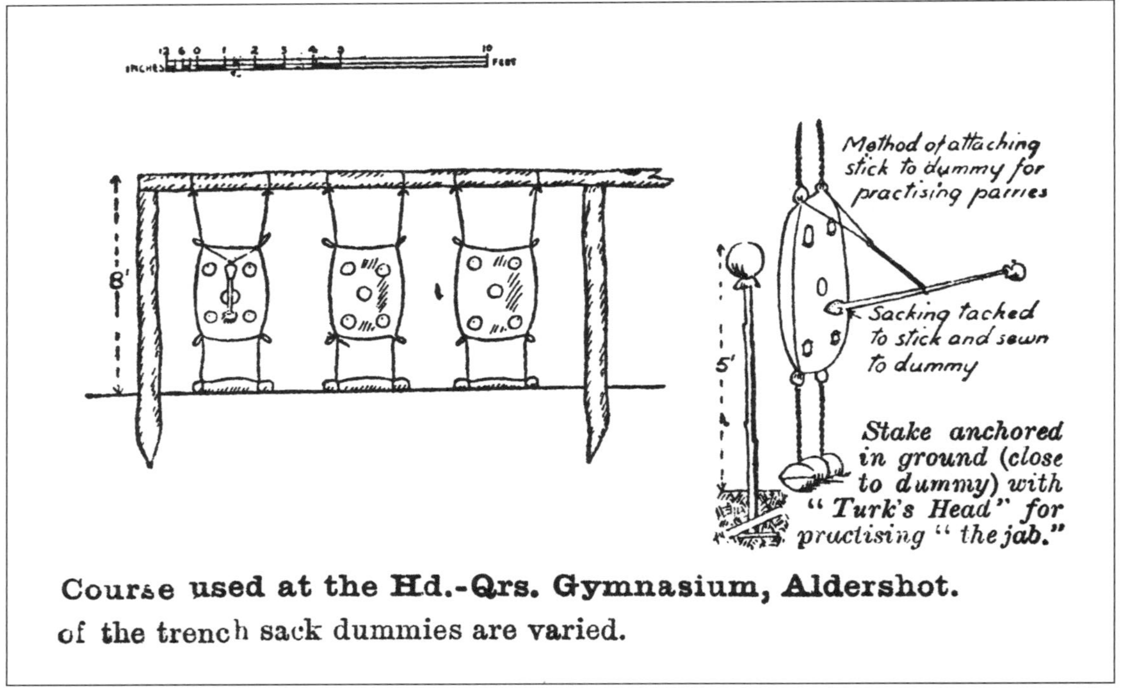


**Course used at the Hd.-Qrs. Gymnasium, Aldershot.**

of the trench sack dummies are varied.

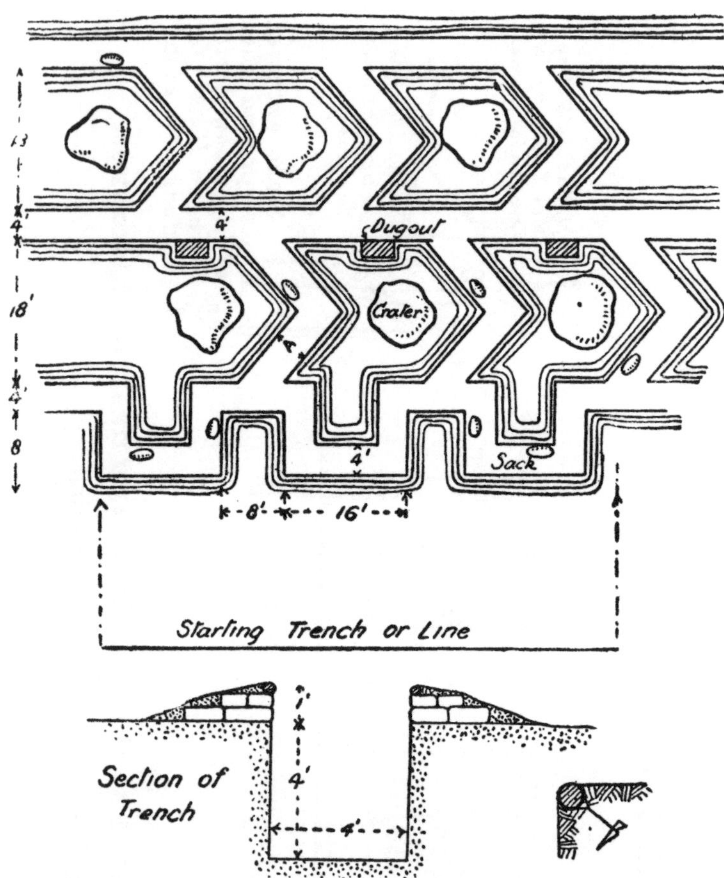


**Diagram 2.—Example of Short Communication Trenches.**

Which should form part of the usual Final Assault Practice course, where, owing to lack of ground, a "labyrinth" for daily practice with the bayonet in the confined space of a trench cannot be constructed within a convenient distance. On arrival in France drafts are tested in trench bayonet work.

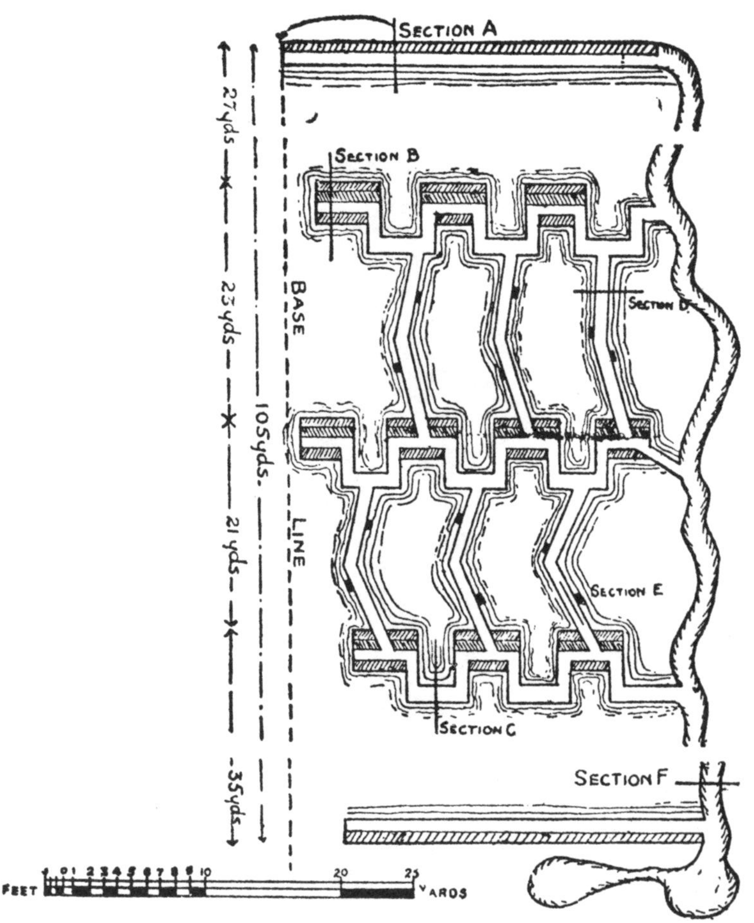


**Diagram 3.—Type of " Nursery " Labyrinth used**

The positions of the sack dummies are frequently changed.

## INSTRUCTIONAL TARGETS

**Fig. 70.**—Solano Instructional Target No. 1. Upright Figure. 25 Yards=400.
(Slightly reduced from actual size. See foot-note, p. 250.)

# I. NAMES OF THE PARTS OF RIFLES—SHORT M.L.E., MARK III, AND CHARGER-LOADING M.L.E.

## (*a*) **Short M.L.E. Mark III** (Figs. 59 and 60).

1. Blade foresight.
2. Foresight block.
3. Band foresight block
4. Key foresight block.
5. Crosspin foresight block
5A. Backsight bed.
6. ,, ,, crosspin.
6A. ,, ,, sight spring screw.
7. Backsight leaf.
8. ,, slide.
9. ,, slide-catch.
10. ,, fine adjustment worm wheel.
10A. Windgauge.
10B. ,, screw.
11. Backsight ramps.
12. Seating for safety-catch.
13. Safety-catch.
14. Locking-bolt stem.
15. Bolt.
16. Bolt-head.
17. Striker.
18. Cocking-piece.
19. Striker collar with stud.
20. Bolt-head tenon.
21. Cocking-piece locking recesses.
22. Locking bolt.
23. ,, ,, flat.
24. ,, ,, thumb-piece.
25. ,, ,, aperture sight stem.
26. ,, ,, stop-pin recesses.
27. ,, ,, safety-catch stem.
28. ,, ,, ,, ,, arm.
29. ,, ,, screw threads.
30. ,, ,, seating.
31. Bolt cam grooves.
32. Sear.
33. ,, seating.
34. ,, spring.
35. Magazine catch.
36. Full bent of cocking-piece
37. Short arm of sear.
38. } Trigger ribs.
39. }
40. Trigger.
41. Trigger axis pin.
41A. Magazine case.
41B. ,, platform spring.
41C. Magazine auxiliary spring.
42. Guard-trigger.
43. Stock fore-end.
44. Spring and stud fore-end.
45. Protector backsight.
46. Handguard front and rear.
47. Spring handguard rear.
48. Lower band groove.
49. Lower band.
50. Nosecap.
51. Protector foresight.
52. Sword bar.
53. Boss for ring of sword-bayonet cross-piece.
54. Swivel seating.
55. ,, piling.
56. Nosecap barrel opening.
57. Inner band.
58. ,, ,, screw.
59. ,, ,, ,, spring.
60. Butt sling swivel.
61. Sword bayonet. pattern '07.
62. Bridge-charger guide.
63. Cut-off.

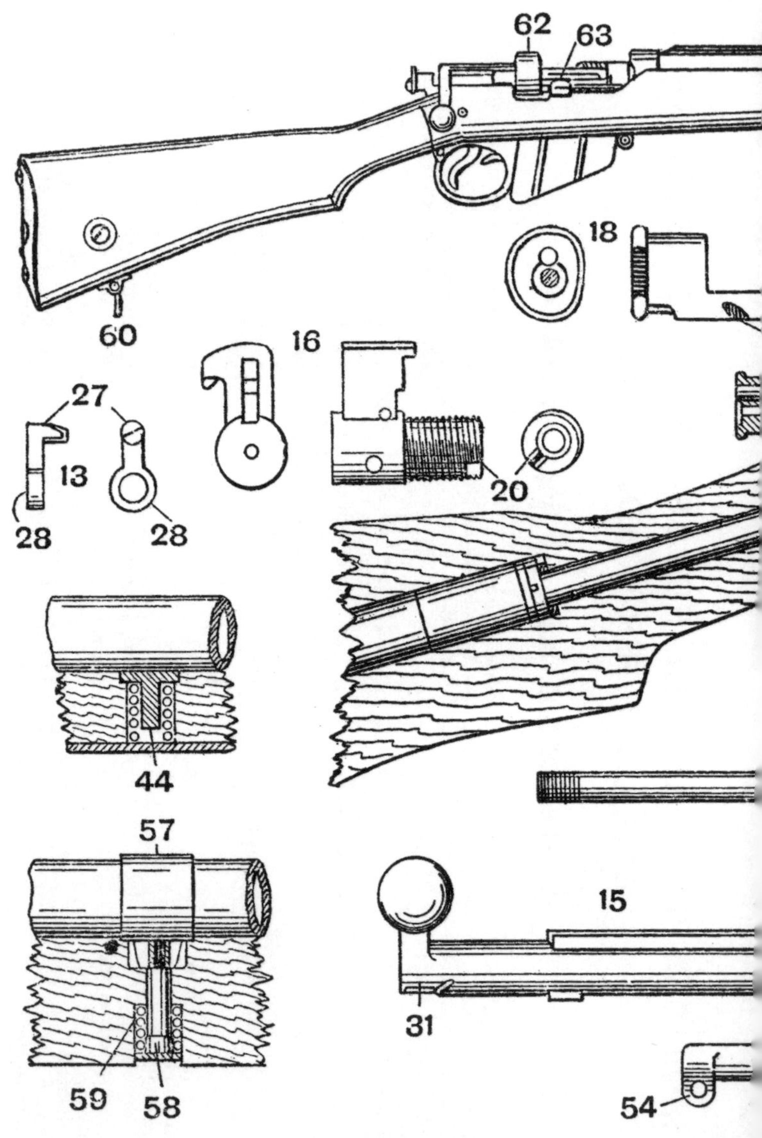


**Fig. 59.**—Short Rifle, Ma

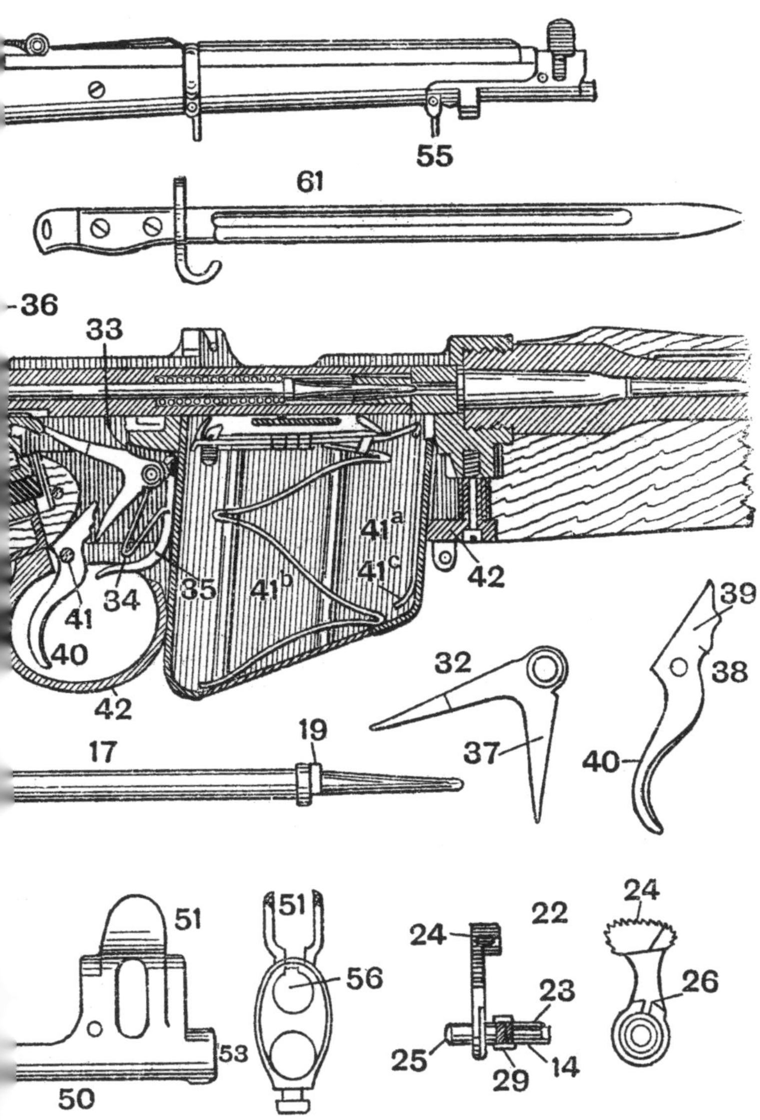


LEE-ENFIELD (MARK III).

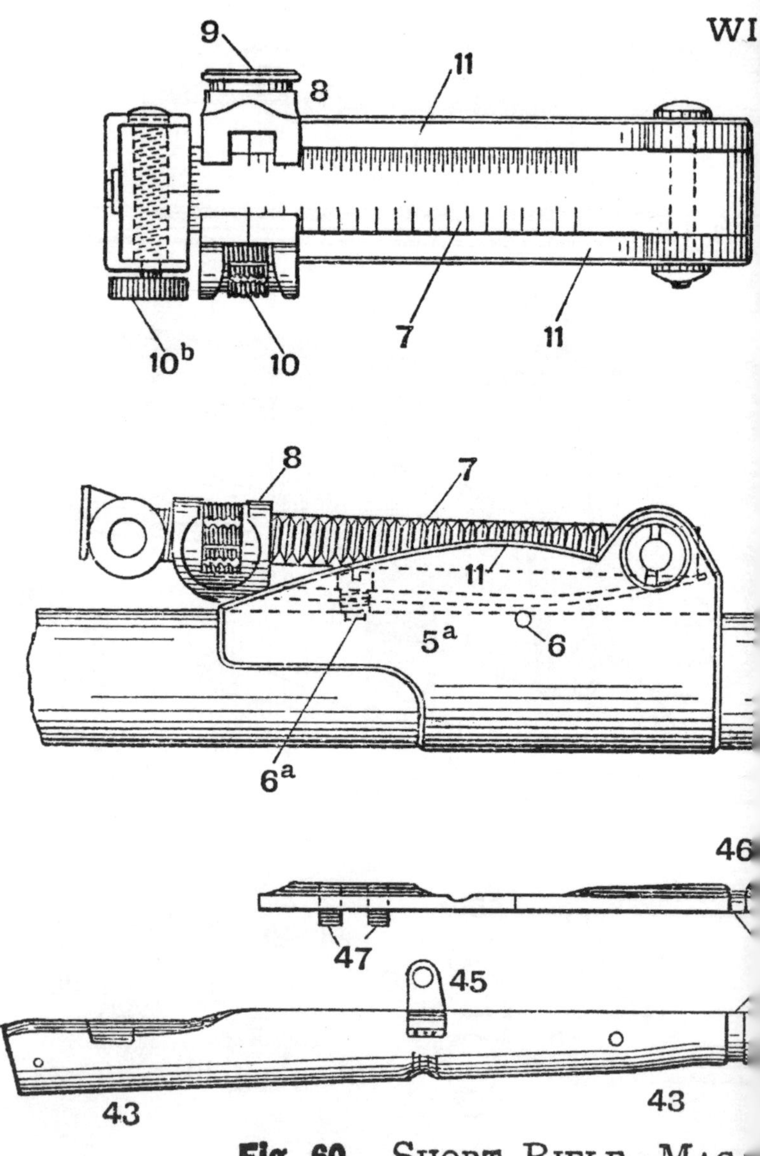


**Fig. 60.**—SHORT RIFLE, MAGA

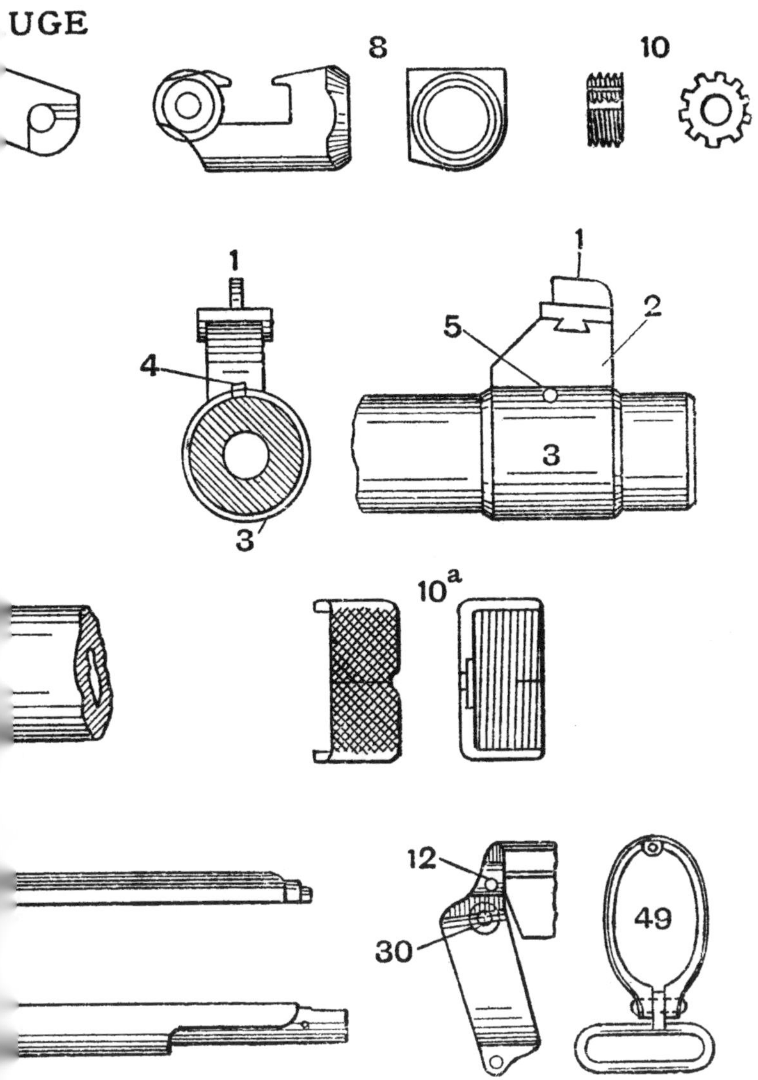


LEE-ENFIELD (MARK III)

## Section 68.—Hand Grenade (Mark I).

**1. General Description** (see Fig. 52).—The grenade consists of the following principal parts: Cap A, body B, detonator C, cane handle D, wood block E, tail F, charge G, and cast-iron ring R.

**2.** The body B of the grenade carries the lyddite charge G. The wood block E is put into the recess in the cup H, and the cup, wood block, and body are then firmly secured together by means of the three brass screws J. Attached to the wood block E is the cane handle D, to the end of which is securely bound the tail F, the cane handle D being for the purpose of throwing the grenade, and the tail F to steady it in flight and to assist to make it travel and fall point foremost.

**3.** The upper part of the body has a groove M formed in it for the purpose of securing the cap A in position. The groove M is provided with four leads into it, two N.N., to allow of the insertion and removal of the cap, and two O.O., to allow the cap to move forward upon the grenade striking the ground or other obstacle. Two projections, e.e., are made in the groove M for the indent X in the cap A to jump when the cap enters or leaves the travel position. One projection is to be made long enough to carry the indent into the *Fire* position. The object of these two projections is to give a definite indication of when the cap is in the *Travel* and *Fire positions. Two indicating knobs* P.P. are secured to the body, and two stop pins Q.Q. are fixed below the indicating knobs P.P., preventing the cap A being pushed down too far (except when turned into the *Fire* position—(see later) if by any accident the safety-pin had been removed or displaced. Fixed to the top of the body are two holding studs R.R. to secure the detonator C when in position. The body has also painted on it in red two arrows L.L. for the purpose of indicating positions of cap A as to the removing, travel, or firing positions.

**4.** The detonator C is formed with a flange S on which are two lugs T.T. for the purpose of turning the detonator when in position, so as to secure it under the heads of the holding studs R.R. On the face of the flange S is fixed a brass plate spring U, for locking the detonator into position. The two grooves V.V. in the flange S of the detonator C are to allow the flange S to pass the holding studs R.R. during insertion or removal of the detonator.

**5.** The cap A carries a steel needle W for firing the detonator. Two small indents X.X. are formed on the cap to engage with the groove M on the body B. The raised lips I.I. are to allow the cap A to clear the indicating knobs P.P. when the cap is being placed or removed from the body of the grenade.

**6.** Two raised lips K.K. are to allow the cap A to move forward when the cap is turned into its firing position, the lips K.K. being raised sufficiently to clear the stop pins Q.Q., this only being possible when the cap is in the firing position. The raised portions Y.Y. are for the indicating knobs to engage with when the cap is turned to the travel position, and thus give a further indication when the cap A is in this position. The cap is also fitted with a safety-pin Z, which passes through the needle and the cap, and prevents the cap moving forward while the pin is in position. The pin Z is secured by a whipcord becket passed over the cap A, and is also further secured by a thin leather strip d passing through a slot at one end, it being necessary to remove both these safeguards before the pin Z can be withdrawn. The safety-pin Z is also passed through the cap A in such a position that if by any mischance the detonator C was not properly secured after being placed in position, the act of placing the cap A on and turning it to the left into the firing position causes the pin Z to engage with the two lugs T.T. on the flange S of the detonator, and automatically locks the detonator under the heads of the holding studs R.R.

**7.** The hook *t* fixed to the body of the grenade is for attaching the latter to the soldier's belt. The grenade with the stick downward is hung on to the belt by the hook.

**8. To Prepare the Grenade for Use.**—(i) Turn the cap A on to the body B to the right until the indicating knobs P.P. are in the raised lips I.I. formed in the cap A. This can be seen by means of the arrows L.L. painted on the body B being opposite the words "remove" on the cap A. Then pull off the cap.

(ii) Place the detonator C in the recess for it. See that the two grooves V.V. in the flange S coincide with the two studs R.R., then press down the detonator into position. When the flange S is home, turn the detonator C to the left, passing the flange under the heads of the studs R.R., and continue turning until the brass plate spring U is released, thus locking the detonator.

(iii) Replace the cap A with the raised lips I.I. over the indicating knobs P.P., and push down into position. After the cap A has been put on, it must be turned one-eighth of a turn to the left, thus bringing the indicating knobs P.P. into the raised positions Y.Y. of the cap A. This is done by pointing the indicating arrows L.L. to "travel" on the cap.

(iv) The grenade is intended to be carried with the raised portions Y.Y. always over the indicating arrows L.L.—*i.e.*, in the travel position, whether the detonator C is in position or not.

(v) **To Throw the Grenade.**—The tail is unwound, and allowed to hang loose at full length.

(vi) The cap is turned from the "travel" to the "fire" position.

(vii) The safety-pin is withdrawn.

(viii) The grenade is thrown by means of the cane D. The latter is grasped between the end furthest from the grenade itself and the attached point of the tail—*i.e.*, on the grooved portion. The grenade is thrown in the required direction either under or over hand, care being taken that the tail cannot entangle itself with the thrower or with any object near him.

(ix) When throwing, the following points should be remembered:

(*a*) The grenade should be thrown well upwards at not less than an angle of about 35 degrees. This, besides assisting in increasing the range to which the grenade can be thrown, renders its action more absolutely certain by causing it to strike the ground nearly vertically. This is especially important when throwing with a following wind.

(*b*) Any obstacle lying between the thrower and the objective must be cleared, as the grenade will almost certainly act on anything it strikes during any part of its flight.

(x) **Caution.**—(i) Should the hand grenade not be used, the cap is to be turned back to "travel" from "fire," the safety-pin (which must be retained) is to be replaced in position, care being taken that the pin passes through the cap, and is secured by passing the whipcord becket over the cap, and by replacing the leather strip *d* through the slot in the end of the safety-pin Z, and the tail rolled up and secured.

(ii) Immediately the grenade has left the hand, the thrower should lie down or get behind cover to reduce the chances of being hit by a splinter, as, of course, the explosion sends these in all directions. Dummy grenades are supplied for practice in throwing.

**9. Use of Grenades.**—In addition to the hand grenade, grenades may be improvised by filling tins with explosive for throwing by hand. Grenades are also constructed so that they can be fired from rifles. Grenades can be used with effect against sap-heads in siege warfare and in trench fighting at close range.

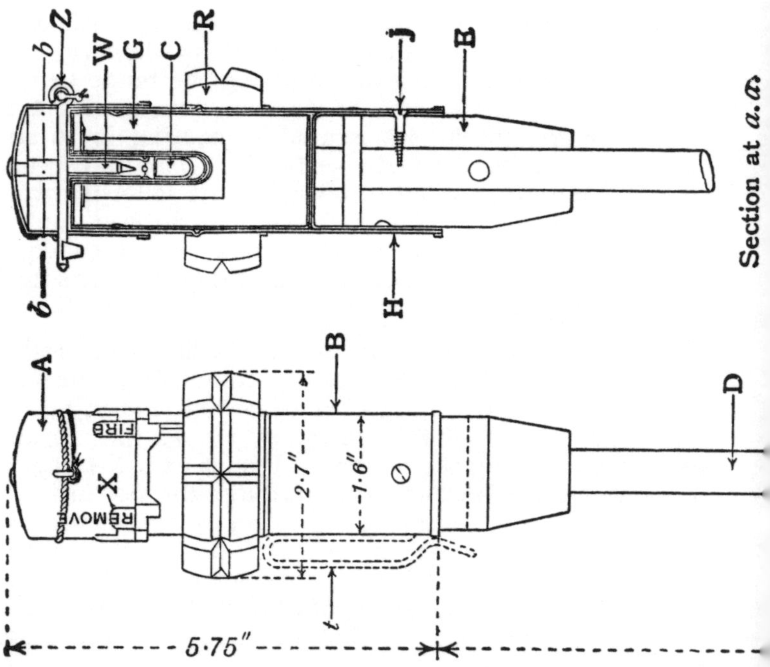


Section at *a.a*

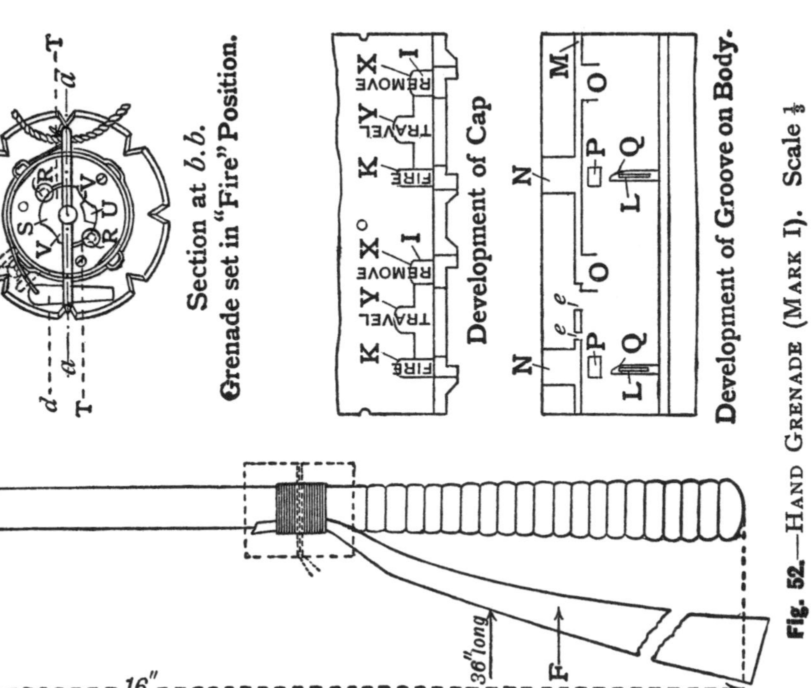


**Fig. 52.**—Hand Grenade (Mark I). Scale $\frac{1}{3}$

The Position "On Guard."

# 4

# MACHINE GUNS

# CHAPTER XV.

## MACHINE GUNS IN BATTLE.

### 158. *Characteristics of machine guns.*

1. A machine gun in action requires a frontage of about two yards. From this narrow front it can deliver a fire equal in volume to that of about 30 men firing rapidly, the frontage required for the latter being at least 15 times as great. It is therefore easier to find a concealed position for a machine gun than for the number of riflemen required to produce an equal volume of fire.

2. When well concealed the gun offers a difficult target, and, as only two men are required for its service, it is not put out of action should these become casualties, provided the remainder of the detachment are trained to take their places.

3. As regards fire effect:—

   i. The effective range of the machine gun may be taken as equal to that of the rifle.

   ii. It has been found by experiment that the fire of a machine gun is about twice as concentrated as that of riflemen firing an equal number of rounds at the same target.

4. In the important matter of control of fire the machine gun has several advantages. Once the gun is loaded and laid, fire can be turned on or off instantaneously; it can be directed as readily as required and can be distributed laterally by traversing.

5. By mounting a few men on the limbered wagon, the guns can be moved rapidly from place to place, while a machine gun with tripod mounting can be taken wherever men on foot can go.

6. On the other hand the machine gun has certain disadvantages as compared with riflemen :—

i. It is more defenceless when on the move, whether carried in the limbered wagon or on pack transport.

ii. Owing to the concentrated nature of its fire as compared with a similar amount of rifle fire, the effect of small errors in aiming or elevation is greater. Thus, a comparatively small error at effective or long ranges will cause the fire of a machine gun to miss altogether a target which would probably be struck by several shots from riflemen making the same error in aim or elevation.

iii. The mechanism of the gun is liable to temporary interruption.

iv. The peculiar noise of the automatic firing attracts attention to the gun, and when steam is given off, owing to the water in the barrel casing boiling, the position of the gun can be readily located unless well concealed.

**159.** *General principles of the employment of infantry machine guns.*

1. The general principles governing the employment of machine guns are based upon the characteristics described in the previous section.

2. (i) The machine gun is a powerful auxiliary to, and well adapted for close co-operation with, infantry.

(ii) The concentrated and accurate nature of its fire, and the speed with which it can be directed on the objective, suits it for the development of surprise effect and covering fire at effective and close infantry ranges.

(iii) The small frontage which it occupies makes it valuable in cramped localities such as salients, villages, roads, or defiles, where it is not possible to deploy a number of rifles. It can also be usefully employed to bring a concentrated enfilade fire to bear on a definite line, such as a hedge, wall, or line of obstacles.

(iv) The power of opening fire at any time when the gun is once laid is valuable on outpost or for night firing, for the gun can command any required locality for any length of time, and it is only necessary to press the double button to produce and apply a large volume of accurate fire at the moment it is required.

(v) The power of turning rapidly in any desired direction, or of "all-round traverse," enables the gun to be brought to bear upon a fresh target without moving the tripod, and with the minimum of movement and exposure. The machine gun can therefore engage quickly an enemy advancing from an unexpected direction without increasing its vulnerability to enfilade fire. This suits it for employment on a flank, in a detached post, or to support infantry in meeting an enveloping attack.

(vi) The power of accompanying infantry in any nature of country is particularly useful in close country. The mobility of the limbered wagons allows the guns to be used to meet unexpected or critical situations so that they may often be usefully employed as a mobile reserve of fire, when they can be moved unseen.

3. The usefulness of the machine gun is limited by its characteristics in the following way :—

i. It is difficult to observe its fire accurately at long ranges, and as compared with field guns its ranging power is limited. It cannot therefore be considered as suitable, normally, for use in place of or as an addition to artillery.

ii. Owing to the concentration of its fire, the expenditure of ammunition is likely to be out of proportion to the results obtained against small or scattered targets such as extended infantry. Unless the range can be ascertained accurately, or the target has considerable depth, effect can only be ensured at ranges of over 1,200 yards by the skilful fire direction of several guns and a heavy expenditure of ammunition.

iii. Owing to the liability of the mechanism to interruption and the expenditure of ammunition involved, the gun is not suited for sustained fire action.

4. To sum up, machine guns are essentially weapons of opportunity. The power of the gun is best used to develop unexpected bursts of fire against favourable targets.

**160.** *The organization and tactical handling of infantry machine guns.*

1. Machine guns are organized in sections, which form an integral part of the battalions to which they belong. But as circumstances will often make it advisable to employ several sections together, a brigade commander may detach two or

more machine gun sections temporarily from their battalions and place them under the brigade machine gun officer (*see* Sec. 8), for employment as a unit of the brigade.

2. When employed by sections with their battalions machine guns are usually better able to take advantage of fleeting opportunities to support infantry closely, and are more easily concealed both on the move and in action, than when brigaded.

On the other hand a single section of these guns cannot be relied upon to obtain results proportionate to the expenditure of ammunition, when first opening fire, at distances beyond about 1,200 yards. Further, it is rarely possible to arrange that sections acting independently shall co-operate effectively with each other.

3. By employing several sections under the control of one commander a brigade commander is able to keep a powerful reserve of fire in hand to be used for any special purpose, the probability of obtaining good effect at ranges beyond 1,200 yards is increased, and it is easier to ensure that the fire is directed on the objective desired by the brigade commander.

4. The disadvantages of brigading machine guns are :—

(i) That the difficulties of concealment are increased.

(ii) That at shorter ranges than 1,000 yards the control of more than one section usually becomes difficult, more especially in attack.

(iii) That the positions suitable for a number of sections in attack are often difficult to find at effective and close ranges, and that the combined movement of a number of sections is only possible under such conditions when the ground is very favourable.

5. It will, therefore, usually depend upon the general situation and upon the ground how many machine guns should be

placed under the control of the brigade machine gun officer, and how many left with the battalions to which they belong.

6. In attack, when the facilities for concealment and control at effective range are good, good results may be obtained by unity of command, and, by a timely concentration of fire, machine guns may be an important factor in the struggle for superiority of fire.

When control and concealment are difficult, or when the brigade is extended over a wide front, it will usually be better to leave guns with their units.

It will often be advisable to employ both methods and to leave their own machine guns with the battalions which are first extended, while those of battalions in reserve are placed under the command of the brigade machine gun officer.

7. Machine guns will usually find opportunities for employment in the attack, in assisting the advance of their infantry by means of covering fire, in protecting attacking infantry against counter-attack or against cavalry, in covering an exposed flank, in assisting the infantry in the fire fight, in preparing for the assault by sudden bursts of fire against the objective of the attack, and in assisting to secure localities seized during the advance. After a successful assault machine guns should reach the captured position as soon as possible in order to pursue the enemy with fire and cover the re-forming of their infantry. In the event of an assault being unsuccessful machine guns should cover the retirement of their own troops, if necessary sacrificing themselves in order to do so.

8. Once in action machine guns should change position as seldom as possible. The difficulties of ranging and of concealment on the move usually outweigh the advantages of decreasing the range.

9. In defence machine guns permanently allotted to the defensive line may lose their mobility, and can rarely be used as a reserve of fire for special purposes, since it is not possible to foresee the action of the enemy when allotting them to their positions. For these reasons it should be exceptional to employ more than a limited number of guns with the firing line in a defensive position. It is better to reconnoitre and prepare machine gun positions, and to keep the bulk of the guns out of action and in hand until an opportunity occurs for using them with a reasonable prospect of decisive effect. It is easy to detach guns where required if they are held in hand, but when distributed and in position it is less easy to collect and withdraw them.

When employed with the firing line in a defensive position, machine guns may be used either dispersed, or brigaded to command approaches, defiles, exits from woods, &c., and to bring fire to bear upon the ground in front of weak parts of the position.

10. When retained as part of a local reserve, machine guns retain their mobility and are therefore available to meet any unexpected situation, or to support local counter attacks closely.

In order to make full use of the guns alternative positions should be allotted to sections. These positions should be thoroughly reconnoitred and all necessary arrangements made for rapid occupation and quick opening of fire.

These arrangements should include :—Previous preparation of cover, information as to the shortest route to the various positions, preparation of range cards, selection of the most suitable position from which to control and observe fire, the most suitable position for the limbered wagons, and arrangements for the supply of ammunition and water.

11. Owing to the liability of the mechanism to interruption, the guns of a section should rarely be employed beyond supporting distance of one another; when sections are acting independently and good cover is not available the guns should usually be not less than 25 yards apart, the average width of the area of ground struck by the bullets of an effective shrapnel.

12. As a general principle no more guns should fire than are necessary to meet the tactical requirements, the remainder being placed in concealed positions ready to open fire on a favourable opportunity or held in positions of readiness under cover according to circumstances. It is, however, of the first importance that sufficient fire effect to attain the object in view should be produced.

13. A machine gun commander should be given definite orders by the commander of the body of troops to which he belongs, as to what is required of him, but he should be allowed as much freedom of action as possible in carrying out these orders, and should be kept informed of all changes and developments of the situation which may affect his action. Initiative and enterprise are essential to the effective handling of machine guns.

14. Machine guns will usually be sufficiently protected by the dispositions of the troops with whom they are acting. Should a machine gun commander find himself in an exposed position, he should apply to the nearest infantry commander for a suitable escort if necessary.

15. When a machine gun is in action only those numbers required to work the gun should be with it. Spare numbers, when not employed as range takers, ground scouts, ammunition carriers, or on similar duties, should be under cover in the vicinity. Groups of men close to machine guns binder the

working of the gun, are apt to disclose its position, and make a vulnerable target.

The limbered wagons will be unpacked in positions where they are screened from the enemy's fire and observation.

The commander of the machine gun section will arrange for the selection of a covered position for his small arm ammunition cart, as close to his guns as possible.

**161.** *Choice of fire positions.*

1. *Reconnaissance.* — Surprise and concealment being important factors in the employment of machine guns, their effective use depends largely upon the skill with which they have been brought into action.

Reconnaissance is therefore of special importance. The brigade machine gun officer if the guns are brigaded, the section officer if they are not, accompanied by range takers and orderlies, should usually be well in advance of his guns, where he can observe the action of the body of infantry with which he is co-operating. He should carefully reconnoitre suitable fire positions and make all preparations for bringing his guns rapidly into action. Alternative positions to which the guns may be moved to meet changes in the situation or to avoid artillery fire should always be selected.

Similar reconnaissances should be carried out, whenever possible, before changing position.

2. The choice of a fire position must depend upon the tactical requirements of the situation, and upon the object in view ; for example, it must depend upon whether it is desired to use covering, enfilade, or flanking fire, or to act by surprise.

In undulating or mountainous country it may be possible to provide covering fire from positions in rear, but in flat country it will rarely be possible to fire over the heads of men in front, and fire positions for machine guns must be sought on the flanks.

Except when affording covering fire from the rear, the gun should be sited as low as is compatible with obtaining the necessary field of fire.

3. A clear field of fire, facilities for observation, a covered approach, concealment and cover for the guns and their detachments, and facilities for ammunition supply, are advantages to be looked for in a good fire position, but one position will rarely unite them all. As a general principle, when the situation calls for effective fire, fire effect must not be sacrificed to obtain concealment.

In arranging for the concealment of the guns it is important to consider the background. The neighbourhood of landmarks and the tops of prominent features should be avoided.

### 162. *General principles of fire control.*

1. The general considerations which govern the selection of a target for machine guns are, its tactical importance, its range, and its vulnerability.

2. Machine guns should rarely open fire except :—

- i. To facilitate movement of their own infantry.
- ii. To prevent or delay movement of the enemy.
- iii. Against a favourable target.

As soon as a machine gun opens fire its presence may be disclosed; its subsequent appearance will then be watched for, and it loses to a great extent the advantage of surprise. Fire should, therefore, not be opened without good reason.

Again, fire should not be opened at ranges beyond 1,200 yards unless a particularly favourable target offers, or a number of guns can be employed (*see* Sec. **160**, 3). Between 1,200 and 800 yards good effect may be anticipated from machine gun fire, and within 800 yards the greatest possible effect should be developed. If the firer can himself obtain observation, the effect of machine gun fire is appreciably increased.

3. Except under special circumstances, as for example when the tactical situation demands the opening of fire irrespective of the probability of obtaining material results in hits, machine guns should open fire only upon targets which are sufficiently large and dense to promise an adequate return for the ammunition expended. Thin lines of infantry in extended order are not a suitable target.

If there is no satisfactory indication of effect, and no special justification for firing at long range exists, it will usually be better to withdraw from action and to seek other opportunities for effective intervention.

4. Machine guns should seldom engage artillery with direct fire beyond close rifle range, for in such circumstances superiority of fire will always rest with the artillery if the machine guns are located. Within close rifle range machine guns, if concealed, should inflict considerable loss on artillery.

5. To sum up, fire should only be opened when probable results will justify it, and the tactical situation demands it. When opened, fire should be maintained so long as there is a reasonable chance of attaining the object for which it was opened. The method and volume of fire must be determined by the tactical situation, the object in view, the nature of the target, the nature of the ground, and the characteristics of the gun.

If these results are to be attained fire must be skilfully controlled and directed by machine gun commanders.

6. When two or more sections are brigaded they will act as a unit under the command of the brigade machine gun officer, who, if the conditions are favourable, *i.e.*, if the sections can be brought into action in such a way that his orders can be heard clearly by all concerned, will direct the fire as regards range, point of aim, method of fire, and the opening and cessation of fire.

It will, however, seldom be possible for a brigade machine gun officer to make his voice heard by more than one section of guns, and the orders for fire direction will usually be limited to indicating the objective by signal or message, and to ordering the opening and cessation of fire, all other details being left to the section officers. High training in semaphore and in the correct passing of orders is essential.

**163.** *Methods of fire.*

1. The principal methods of fire are :—

   i. Ranging fire.
   ii. Rapid fire.
   iii. Traversing fire.

i. In *Ranging fire* groups of from 10 to 20 rounds are used to obtain observation. When the conditions for observation are favourable a group of 10 rounds should be sufficient. Under less favourable conditions, groups of as many as 20 rounds may be necessary, but if observation is not then obtained it is unlikely to be obtained with larger groups. Single deliberate shots are of no value for ranging. Ranging fire should never be used when surprise is of importance.

ii. *Rapid fire* is used when the greatest volume of fire is required. It is produced and applied by means of a series of long groups of from 30 to 50 rounds. The firer pauses momentarily between each group to ensure that the sights are correctly aligned, and continues until ordered to cease fire or until he considers it necessary to do so. Rapid fire will be used (1) when the sighting elevation has been successfully obtained by ranging fire; (2) when surprise effect is required; (3) with combined sights.

iii. *Traversing fire.*—This method is employed against a linear target, and is applied by means of a series of small groups with the object of covering as wide a front as possible with only sufficient volume to ensure effect. In this case a group should consist of from 5 to 10 rounds only, because against a linear target greater volume will not produce greater effect. (*See also* Sec. **103,** 10.) Traversing may be either horizontal or diagonal.

2. *Combined sights.*—When two or more guns are working together, the depth of the effective zone can be increased by ordering different elevations to be used by each gun, while each uses the same aiming mark. By this means, while the effective zone is increased, the density of fire is considerably reduced. The difference of elevation used depends chiefly on the number of guns available For general guidance, when one section only is available, combined sights differing by 100 yards should be used at and beyond 800 yards and up to 1,200 yards inclusive; beyond 1,200 yards the difference in sighting should not exceed 50 yards between guns. With two or more sections the difference of sighting between guns should not exceed 50 yards. When both guns of a section are sighted to the same elevation, "combined sights by sections," differing by 100 yards may be used.

Combined sights should at once be discontinued if accurate observation of the strike of bullets can be obtained.

Machine gun commanders when ordering combined sights will give out the lowest range and the difference in sighting to be used. The lowest range will always be taken by the left hand gun of the section or sections as the case may be. The No. 1 of that gun will pass to the No. 1 of the gun on his right the range he himself is using and the difference ordered, and so on down the line.

When the target to be engaged is a narrow one, and all guns are using the same aiming mark, it will generally be impossible for the firers to observe their own particular cone of fire. In these circumstances no alteration in sighting is permissible except under the orders of the machine gun commander. In other circumstances, *i.e.*, when the guns are laid on different points of aim, each firer should endeavour to correct his elevation from observation of the bullet strike. In such cases the effect may be increased by traversing from the flanks inwards, or from the centre outwards. If, as a result of his observations or for other reasons, the machine gun commander wishes to alter the sighting, the quickest method is to bring the elevation of the left hand gun above that of the right hand gun or to lower the elevation of the right hand gun below that of the left hand gun according as to whether he wishes to increase or decrease the elevation. If the machine gun commander is directing the fire from the opposite flank to that of the gun or guns whose elevation he wishes to alter, it will be necessary to cease firing momentarily for his order to be received, after which he will immediately give the signal to continue. This will often not be necessary when he is on the same flank.

### 164. *Signals.*

1. In many cases observation will be impossible from the gun position, and it will be necessary for observers to signal results from a flank.

The following semaphore code is used in signalling the results of observation of fire :—

P = Plus : meaning fire observed at least 50 yards beyond target.

M = Minus : meaning fire observed at least 50 yards short of target.

T = Right : meaning fire observed to right of target.

L = Left : „ „ „ to left of target.

C = Centre : „ direction of fire correct.

U = Unobserved : meaning no observation obtained.

Q = Query : meaning fire observed but its position uncertain.

R = Range : meaning range correct.

2. The signaller at the observation post should give the "call up" to show that the observers are ready. "P"; and "M" may be repeated for multiples of 50 yards, thus "P P" would mean, "fire observed at least 100 yards beyond target." Signals should be repeated from the gun position if this can be done without disclosing the position to the enemy.

3. On all occasions when guns are firing, the following signals should be used in controlling fire :—

Signal for "action."—Both arms, fully extended, raised from the sides to a position in line with the shoulders and lowered again. This motion to be repeated until it is seen that the signal is being complied with.

Signal for "out of action."—Arms swung in a circular motion in front of the body.

By No. 2. Hand up = Gun ready to open fire.

By Controlling Officer. Hand up = Preparatory to opening fire.

Hand dropped = Open fire.

Elbow close to the side, forearm waved horizontally = Cease fire.

Other signals as in Sec. **94.**

# 5

# UNIFORMS & EQUIPMENT

*The War Budget,*
*October 7th, 1915.*

3D THIS CASH COUPON will be accep'ed as cash in part payment to the value of 3d. for the Regimental Badges offered by the "War Budget." (No. W.B. 014.) CUT THIS COUPON OUT.

ii.

# COMPLETE EQUIPMENT FOR THE FIELD

**THE SOLDIER'S KNAPSACK CONTAINS:**

Waterproof Sheet, Overcoat, Pairs of Socks, Mess Tins, Knife, Fork and Spoon, Hair Brush, Comb, Tooth Brush, Soap and Towel, Housewife, Razor, Shaving Brush, and Shirt, all of which are supplied on joining by Army authorities, but there are several other articles which are not supplied, and some of these will be found mentioned in the panels below.

***The Soldier's Match-Box.***

BRYANT & MAY'S

**"SERVICE" MATCH-BOX COVER** (Reg. Design 642237.)

Nickel ... ... ... 1s. each
Dull Black Finish... ... 4½d. each
Postage 1d. extra.

Obtainable of Outfitters, Stores, Tobacconists, etc., or Direct from

**BRYANT & MAY, Ltd.,** (Dept. W.B.), Fairfield Works, Bow, London, E.

**GUN DEAFNESS PREVENTED**

DEAFNESS IS A TRIAL THAT CANNOT BE BORNE PATIENTLY. There are many men home from the Front suffering keenly from this affliction, which is easily prevented by the use of HARBUTT'S PATENT

**FIBROUS PLASTICINE**

A small piece made into a plug and placed in each ear effectually cuts up the nerve shattering concussions while interfering but little with ordinary conversation, the word of command, or the bugle call; and the price is only 7d., in a strong tin box, post paid; larger boxes 1s. 8d., post paid. Every man at the front ought to have a box. Send one to your friend there. Postage abroad 3d. extra for the small box and 9d. extra on the large.

HARBUTT'S PLASTICINE, Ltd., 24, Bathampton, BATH

**Soldiers and Sailors need Handkerchiefs.**

**Give them**

TWO GOLD MEDALS.

**EXCELDA HANDKERCHIEFS**

A genuine, durable, and satisfactory article—soft and ready for use, 6½d. each

**"VERMIJELLI"**

has now been proved by use in the Army, and by thousands of other users to be the only efficacious remedy for LICE, FLEAS, and other VERMIN.

IT IS NON-POISONOUS, NON-INFLAMMABLE, and MIXES WITH WATER and Possesses many special advantages.

Full particulars can be obtained from SOLE MANUFACTURERS:

**S. BOWLEY & SON,** Wellington Works, Battersea Bridge, **LONDON, S.W.**

**Make your Wrist Watch break-proof'**

Every wrist-watch wearer—soldier or sportsman—needs the **Army Protector** which converts **any** wrist watch into a miniature hunter guarding the glass and case from breakage, protecting the wearer from the danger of splinters, and preventing dangerous reflections from the glass.

**The ARMY WRIST WATCH PROTECTOR**

Nickel or Khaki Finish, 1/6. Leather Covered, 2/6. Solid Silver, from 6/6. Also in Solid Gold.

*Sold by Jewellers, Silversmiths, Cutlers, or obtainable direct from Sales Manager.*

Waltham Bldgs., 29 Church St., Liverpool.

AMMUNITION POUCHES

ENTRENCHING TOOL

WATER BOTTLE

HANDLE OF ENTRENCHING TOOL

"DRI-PED" SOLE LEATHER KEEPS HIS FEET DRY ALWAYS

***Lance-Corp'l Edward Dwyer, V.C. writes:—***

"Wounds and nerves are only some of the troubles of the trenches, wet and swollen feet are the limit. The terrible banging of the guns you get used to, but if your feet are bad life's a misery. I got a straight tip from a pal before going into the trenches. My pal sold me some "Dri-ped" soles to fix to my boots. A lot of chaps are wearing them. I must say it was money well spent, they're simply grand and keep your feet fine and dry, even in the wettest trenches.

"LANCE-CORP'L EDWARD DWYER, V.C., 1st East Surrey Regt."

"Dri-ped" Sole Leather is nearly as tough and enduring as Tommy himself; and even the mud of Flanders didn't penetrate the "Dri-ped" Soles worn by thousands of men at the Front during last winter.

Get the double-wearing, wet-resisting "Dri-ped"—on new or re-soled footwear—for "civi" or soldier—from dealers and repairers everywhere.

*Send a postcard for interesting free booklet "How to Double Boot Life"—list sent free of dealers and repairers stocking 'Dri-ped' in your district. Write now, to William Walker & Sons, Ltd., County Buildings, Cannon Street, Manchester.*

DRI-PED REGD

See this stamp in purple every few inches on each sole—without it, the leather is a substitute.

**DRI-PED** Regd

**THE SUPER-LEATHER FOR SOLES**

# WHAT TO SEND TO GERMANY

Readers of "THE WAR BUDGET" who have relatives or friends in any of the German (or Holland, etc.,) detention camps, can send parcels direct through the Post free of all charges.

Parcels should be addressed as follows:

Name (in full) ..........................................................
Rank and Regiment.......................................................
British Prisoner of War interned in Germany (or Holland, etc.),
c/o General Post Office,
Mount Pleasant, London.

N.B.—In the case of Civilian Prisoners of War, the places of detention should be shown in the address.

Parcels may be handed in at any Post Office in the ordinary way.

From messages received from prisoners of war, we learn that many lack even the actual necessities of life, and the people at home render a national service by opening their purses and sending parcels of comforts to the brave officers and men who are suffering dire privation in the hands of the enemy.

## FOOD FOR PRISONERS OF WAR

If your soldier friend or relative is a Prisoner of War in Germany, he will appreciate

**A PARCEL OF FOOD FROM HOME**

more than anything else. Therefore write to us To-Day for a copy of our Complete List of Provision Parcels, each article is in a separate air-tight tin, and Guaranteed of the Best Quality. The prices of these parcels are:—**5s., 7s. 6d., 10s. 15s., and 20s.**

**SEND US A POSTAL ORDER FOR 5s.**

**With the full address of the one to whom you require a parcel sent**, we will forward him at once securely packed and properly declared for Customs purposes, a parcel containing the following:—

| | |
|---|---|
| 1lb. TIN BISCUITS (Plain). | ½lb. TIN BUTTER. |
| 1lb. TIN CHEESE. | 1lb. TIN MARMALADE. |
| ½lb. TIN CAFE AU LAIT. | 1 GLASS MEAT PASTE. |
| 1 TIN SARDINES. | 1 TIN OPENER. |

We will at the same time advise him that it has been sent, by means of a special post card, printed in both English and German; on which is included the address of the sender, so that he can acknowledge its receipt direct.

*Post your order to-day to—*

**HUDSON BROS., LTD.** (MILITARY HOME SUPPLIES DEPT.),
**34, FARRINGDON ROAD, LONDON, E.C.**
*Branches throughout London and Provinces.*

## Make HIM Happy

Nothing could be more acceptable to your Soldier or Sailor friend — whether a Prisoner of War or with the Fighting Forces — than a generous supply of Wrigley's SPEARMINT Chewing Gum.

Allays thirst, renders the mouth cool and sweet, prevents fatigue, soothes the nerves and aids digestion. A very welcome change from Chocolate or Cigarettes.

**WRIGLEY'S** SPEARMINT
**CHEWING GUM**

Send him some to-day. **It MUST be Wrigley's.**
He needs it badly.

**MAMMOTH BOX** Containing 40 Bars **1/6**

Larger quantities are supplied as follows:— Box containing 20 packets of 5 bars each, 4s.; 10 boxes (enough for 1,000 men), 35s. Wrigley's enjoys the largest sale of any chewing gum in the World (guaranteed pure and harmless), obtainable from all Chemists and Confectioners. Should any difficulty be experienced, write direct to—

**WRIGLEY'S Ltd., Lambeth Palace Road, S.E.**

## They MUST Eat— They Enjoy Washing— and *DON'T* they Enjoy Good Reading!

Our boys in Germany want good reading even more than the boys in training, or at the front —and *they* clamour for it, as you know.

Here are just the rattling good stories to keep them cheery:—

"Battle," by W. Douglas Newton
"For England," by Morice Gerard
"This Man and This Woman," by L. Clarke
"Love Tides," by Captain Frank H. Shaw
(Price 3d. each volume).

***SPECIAL OFFER***

All four will be sent post free to any man on Active service or British prisoner in Germany, upon receipt of his name and address and One Shilling, by "Lloyd's News" Home Novels, 12, Salisbury Square, London, E.C.

128 pages each. In Three-Coloured Covers

**SEND YOUR FRIENDS**

## BRAND'S MEAT LOZENGES

**(PURE BEEF)**

WORLD - RENOWNED
for their sustaining properties.

***"A Meal in the Vest Pocket"***

No more acceptable gift can be made to officers and men

**IN BOXES 1/-, 1/6 & 2/9, of Chemists and Stores or direct of—**

**BRAND & CO., LTD.,**
**Mayfair Works, Vauxhall, London, S.W.**

By Royal Letters Patent. Patented throughout the World.

# THE "ANGELO" Shirt

## for War Service

A glance at the illustrations will show you how immensely superior the "Angelo" is to any other shirt hitherto invented. However strenuous the work or long the march the

**"Angelo" cannot "ruck" or "creep" up**

thus assuring comfort all the time.

The lappet makes the difference. This shaped back shirt or lappet draws right through to the front, and is held securely and simply in position by adjustable suspenders. It is thus impossible to "creep." In addition it is highly hygienic and protects the vital parts from damp, chills, etc.

*Portion of Uniform removed to show special feature of the "Angelo."*

Same in price and appearance as an ordinary shirt, but always snugly fitting and incomparably more comfortable. Can be worn with or without braces.

*Front view showing lappet attached to brace bar.*

**INVALUABLE TO HORSEMEN, CYCLISTS, OR KILTED REGIMENTS**

The "Angelo" Shirt is obtainable from outfitters everywhere, in all classes of material, Khaki, Wool, etc., or direct from

**ANGELO SHIRT CO. LTD., London, Glasgow, and 28 North Bridge, Edinburgh.**

**Price 6/6 post paid**

**Officers' Service Shirts. Best quality, 14/6 to measure.**

IN FULL FIGHTING ORDER AND EQUIPPED FOR EVERY EMERGENCY.—THE BRI

THIS GRAPHIC PORTRAYAL OF EVERYTHING AN INFANTRYMAN CARRIES ON ACTIVE SERVICE WILL ASTONISH MANY WHO HAVE JACKET SERVED OUT TO OUR TROOPS IS AN ADDITIONAL ITEM,

LDIER'S BURDEN IN THE FIRING-LINE PICTURED FROM A TO Z.

GUE IDEA OF THE QUANTITY OF ARTICLES INCLUDED IN THE EQUIPMENT OF A SOLDIER OF THE LINE. THE WINTER GOATSKIN TIMES HE CARRIES ALSO EXTRA RATIONS AND FUEL.

**BADGES OF RANK: HOW TO DISTINGUISH BRITISH OFFICERS.**

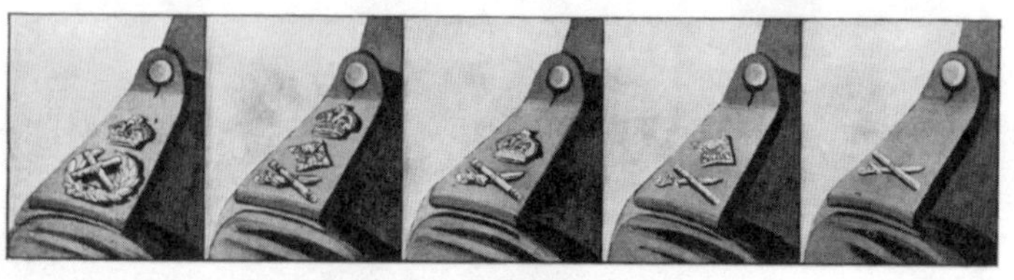

ON THE SHOULDER STRAP

Crossed batons on a wreath of laurel with a crown above indicate
**A Field-Marshal**

Crossed sword and baton with a crown and star above indicate
**A General**

Crossed sword and baton with a crown above indicate
**A Lieut.-General**

Crossed sword and baton with a star above indicate
**A Major-General**

Crossed sword and baton alone indicate
**A Brigadier-General**

ON CUFFS

A crown and two stars indicate
**A Colonel**

A crown and one star indicate
**A Lieut.-Colonel**

A crown alone indicates
**A Major**

Three stars indicate
**A Captain**

Two stars indicate
**A Lieutenant**

One star only indicates
**A Second Lieutenant**

ON THE ARM (NON-COMMISSIONED OFFICERS)

A crown, crossed swords, bugles, and three stripes, indicate
**Colour-Sergeant**
(Rifle Regiment)

A crown, crossed flags, and three stripes, indicate
**Colour-Sergeant**

A crown and three stripes indicate
**Company Sergeant-Major**

Three stripes indicate
**Sergeant**

Two stripes indicate
**Corporal**

One stripe indicates
**Lance-Corporal**

# BENSON'S

## LUMINOUS

## *"Active Service" Watch.*

**VISIBLE AT NIGHT.**

**WARRANTED TIMEKEEPERS.**

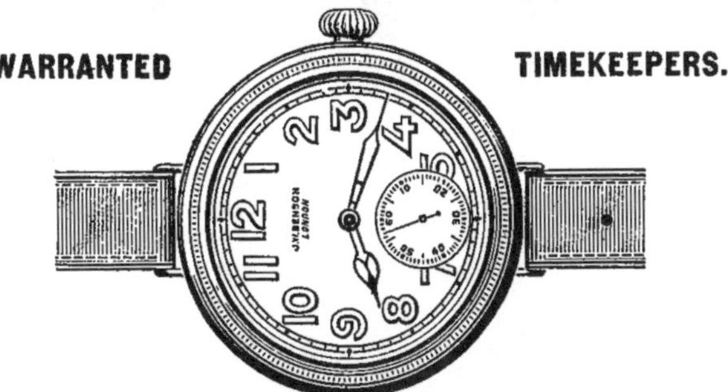

Fine quality lever movement, fully luminous figures and hands, and extra heavy Screw Case (special to our make), Crystal Glass, **£3 3s.**; Gold, **£8.** Hunter or Half-Hunter, Silver, **£3 15s.**; Gold, **£8 10s.** Others in Silver, from **£2 10s.**; or Gold, from **£6.**

*Illustrated Lists of Wristlet Watches, Rings (with size card), Watches, Chains, Jewels, etc., post free.*

**62 & 64, LUDGATE HILL, E.C.4,**

**and 25, OLD BOND STREET, W.1.**

TRADE MARK
GEO. CORDING LTD.
GUARANTEED
WATERPROOFS
By Appointment
To H.M. THE KING.
WATERPROOF
TRENCH COAT
LIGHTWEIGHT ... Price 90/-
MEDIUM or HEAVY „ 105/-
FLEECE LININGS ... 45/-
Write giving chest measure and length.
CAMP AND
HOSPITAL EQUIPMENT
WATERPROOF
BOOTS & WADERS
OILSKINS
'Phone.: Regent 3738.
Gerrard 6327.
CEO. CORDING LTD.
125 REGENT STREET, AND
16 NEW BOND ST., LONDON, W.1.

***FOR THE TRENCHES.***

**BRYANT & MAY'S**

# 'KAMPITE'

## SAFETY TRENCH COOKER

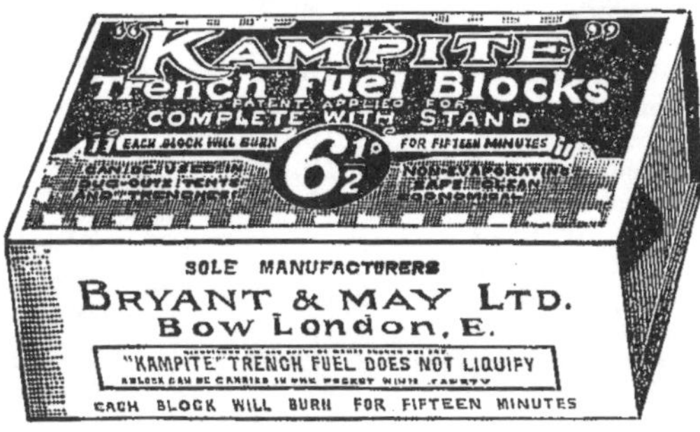


**NO SPIRIT** **NO LIQUID**

**SAFE, CLEAN & RELIABLE**

Complete with collapsible stand and six fuel blocks.

**BRYANT & MAY, LTD., LONDON & LIVERPOOL**

**134 to 140 Oxford St., London, W**

ESTABLISHED NEARLY A CENTURY.

# Field Service Outfits

| | | | |
|---|---|---|---|
| ***First quality Whipcord or Serge*** | | | |
| **Field Service Jacket ..** | **£3** | **0** | **0** |
| **Slacks to match .. ..** | **1** | **5** | **0** |
| ***Second quality Serge*** | | | |
| **Field Service Jacket ..** | **2** | **15** | **0** |
| **Slacks to match .. ..** | **1** | **1** | **0** |
| **Khaki Breeches .. ..** | **1** | **10** | **0** |
| **Field Service Great Coat** | **3** | **10** | **0** |
| **British Warm Coat ..** | **2** | **15** | **0** |
| **Bedford Cord Breeches ..** | **1** | **7** | **6** |
| **Bedford Cord Riding Pantaloons, Strapped Doe ..** | **2** | **10** | **0** |
| **Regulation Rain Coat ..** | **2** | **15** | **0** |
| **Sam Browne Belt, complete** | **2** | **2** | **0** |
| **Field Service Cap.. ..** | | **12** | **6** |
| **New Soft Trench Cap ..** | | **14** | **6** |
| ***Mediterranean Drill*** | | | |
| **Field Service Jacket ..** | **1** | **15** | **0** |
| **Slacks .. .. ..** | | **13** | **0** |
| **Shorts .. .. ..** | | **10** | **6** |
| **Breeches .. .. ..** | **1** | **5** | **0** |

**Badges Extra.**

## CAMP EQUIPMENT

*Write or call for full Price List.*

# Comforts *for* Campaigners

THE comfort of a man in the trenches depends very largely upon his friends at home. If they send him the things necessary, well and good; if not, remember there are no Chemists' Shops in the trenches.

Boots The Chemists

## "TINNED HEAT"
(SOLID METHYLATED SPIRIT)

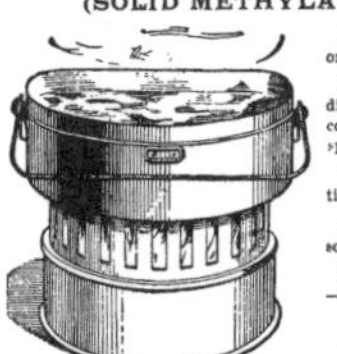

Is a little round tin pocket stove or Campaigner's Cooker.

It measures but 3½ inches in diameter and 1¼ inches high, and contains solidified methylated spirit.

It is perfectly safe—quite practical and absolutely efficient.

It is an ideal arrangement for soldiers' use in the trenches.

It lights instantly—burns readily—simplicity itself to use.

Price **10½d.** each.

Boots The Chemists

COMPRESSED
## TEA TABLETS

The tablets are most convenient to carry and to use; all that is necessary is to drop two or three of the tablets in a cup, pour boiling water on them, and add sugar and milk to taste.

The tablets consist of the purest young leaves of the finest qualities of tea—compressed—that's all. Nothing is added, and absolute purity is guaranteed. The blending—choice aroma and subtle flavour—will be appreciated by all tea-lovers, while the comparative freedom from tannin makes Boots *The* Chemists' Tea Tablets ideal for dyspeptics and invalids.

50 Tablets **5d.** 100 **9d.** 200 **1/6**

Boots The Chemists

## VERMIN POWDER

Boots The Chemists
SPECIAL PREPARATION AGAINST
VERMIN IN THE TRENCHES
Directions for Use

FOR THE PEST OF THE TRENCHES

Men who at home are used to immaculate cleanliness, and to whom the thought of a single one of these pests on their bodies would, ordinarily, be revolting, cannot get away from the attentions of body parasites whilst serving with the colours in France and Belgium.

Officers and men alike are troubled with these disgusting vermin, unless an application be used to destroy and prevent their existence on the clothing or person.

Boots Vermin Powder is the preparation that does that and THOROUGHLY TOO. In spite of imitations galore, it is still the best. It is like Toilet Powder to look at and to use. It is cleanly, efficient, and is supplied in a sprinkler tin for convenient and economical use.

Price **9d.** per tin.

Boots The Chemists

## ANTI-FLY CREAM

Prevents the bites and stings of mosquitoes, flies, and insects, and is soothing where such have occurred.

Irritating as the fly is at home, in France, Belgium, and in Egypt there are just millions of these winged pests worrying our soldiers.

Boots *The* Chemists **ANTI-FLY CREAM** means a sure escape from fly and mosquito trouble.

Numerous testimonials received from the front prove that Boots *The* Chemists **ANTI-FLY CREAM** has been of the highest service to our men.

It is pleasant, clean, safe, and satisfactory.

Price **9d.** per Tube. Trial Tin **4½d.**

Boots The Chemists

### FOOT COMFORT

fully merits its title. It gives relief to tired, weary and aching feet, and makes such conditions a thing of the past.

Invaluable to "marching men."

Price **3d.** per tin.

Boots The Chemists

### SHAVING STICKS

are deliciously soothing to the most sensitive skin. They give a lasting lather with cold water, and are delicately perfumed.

Price in Leatherette Case **4½d.** Larger size in Metal Case **8½d.**

Boots The Chemists

### PEPPERMINT TABLETS

are very strong in flavour.

A comfort indeed, and used by soldiers in place of tobacco. Very stimulating. Vest pocket size tins.

Price **3d.** per tin.

Boots The Chemists

### MELOIDS
FOR THE THROAT

are concentrated black pellets of a liquorice-menthol flavour. Splendid protectors against the ravages of cold and damp.

Price **3d.** per tin.

*Principal London Branches:*

**182 REGENT STREET, W.**

**112-118 EDGWARE ROAD.**

OVER 100 BRANCHES IN AND AROUND LONDON.

555 Branches in Town and Country.

iv. ADVERTISEMENT. *The War Budget, October 7th, 1915*

# EACH ONE OF THAT VAST NUMBER

who has answered his country's call would be happier, safer and better fitted to meet many dangers, if equipped with the comforts and necessities specially manufactured for campaigners by Boots *The* Chemists.

Here are some of them:

## Boots The Chemists
## Water Sterilizers

One of the most dreadful of all campaign dangers is impure water.

Boots *The* Chemists manufacture and supply Tablets for Sterilizing and Purifying water for drinking purposes.

A shilling bottle contains 50 tablets, sufficient for the complete sterilization of 50 pints of water.

The tablets impart an agreeable lemon flavour to water and render it a pleasant, safe, thirst quenching drink.

It is a scientific fact that two of these tablets dropped into the ordinary service bottle and allowed to stand for half-an-hour will absolutely destroy the germs of typhoid.

**Price 1/- Per Bottle of 50 Tablets.**

At all the 555 Branches of Boots **The** Chemists. Post free 3d. extra from Boots **The** Chemists, M.O., Nottingham.

## Boots The Chemists
## ANTI-FLY CREAM

Prevents the bites and stings of mosquitoes, flies, and insects, and is soothing where such have occurred.

Irritating as the fly is at home, in France, Belgium, in the Gallipoli and in Egypt there are just millions of these winged pests worrying our soldiers.

Boots *The* Chemists Anti-Fly Cream means a sure escape from fly and mosquito trouble.

Numerous testimonials received from the front prove that Boots *The* Chemists Anti-Fly Cream has been of the highest service to our men.

It is pleasant, clean, safe and satisfactory.

**Per Tube 9d. Trial Tin 4½d.**

At all the 555 Branches of Boots **The** Chemists Post free 1d. extra from Boots **The** Chemists, M.O., Nottingham.

## Boots The Chemists
## VERMIN POWDER

In times of war the plague of body vermin is invariably present with those on field service.

Ordinary washing, even with boiling water, will not clear these pests from the clothing or person.

The annoyance and hardship is suffered by both officers and men in the field, preventing sleep and acting injuriously on both the physical and mental being of the men.

Boots *The* Chemists Vermin Powder, scientifically compounded, *is successful*, convenient, cleanly and absolutely harmless.

**Price 9d. Per Box.**

At all the 555 Branches of Boots **The** Chemists.

Post free 1d. extra from Boots **The** Chemists, M.O. Nottingham.

## Boots The Chemists
## IODINE TUBES OR AMPOULES

IODINE AMPOULES are little glass tubes, hermetically sealed, containing Iodine Tincture, in either 2½ p.c. or 5 p.c. strengths.

Medical men are united in urging the instant application of a bactericide to all wounds.

Iodine Ampoules are convenient to carry—simplicity itself to use.

When the end of an Ampoule is snapped, a lint swab becomes saturated with Iodine, which is then painted on the affected part.

Many thousands of these Ampoules have been sent to our Troops.

Single Ampoule in protective metal case. **3d.** Flat Metal Box containing six Ampoules. **1/3**

At all the 555 Branches of Boots **The** Chemists. Post free 1d. extra from Boots **The** Chemists, M.O., Nottingham.

## Boots The Chemists
## FOOT COMFORT

No soldier can perform his duties, or retain his health, or anything like a semblance of comfort, should he suffer the aches and agonies of foot trouble. Boots Foot Comfort preparation gives instant relief to tired, weary, aching feet, and is indispensable to men on the march.

**In Tins 3d. Each.**

"I take this opportunity of expressing to you my complete satisfaction of the preparation called 'Foot Comfort.'"

"For the last six weeks I have been in camp, and during that time I have daily used your 'Foot Comfort,' which has invariably relieved my feet when tired from marching."

At all the 555 Branches of Boots **The** Chemists.

Post Free 1d. extra from Boots **The** Chemists, M.O., Nottingham.

## Boots The Chemists
## SHAVING STICKS

The soldier at the front feels lost without shaving soap.

Boots Shaving Sticks are the best to send to him.

They are deliciously soothing to the most sensitive skin. They give a creamy, lasting, abundant lather, even with cold water. Manufactured from the purest ingredients, delicately perfumed, Boots Shaving Sticks are indeed exceptional value.

In neat leatherette case **4½d.** Larger size in screw-capped metal tube **8½d.**

At all the 555 Branches of Boots **The** Chemists.

Post free 1d. extra from Boots **The** Chemists, M.O., Nottingham.

*Principal London Branches:*

**182, REGENT STREET, W.**
**112-118, EDGWARE RD., W.**

**Over 100 Branches in and around London. ::: 555 Branches in Town and Country.**

*(Boots Pure Drug Co., Ltd.)*

Printed by St. Clements Press, Ltd., and Published by the "DAILY CHRONICLE," 12, Salisbury Square, London, E.C.

# The Campaigner Who Knows

Makes Fry's Pure Breakfast Cocoa his favourite Beverage whenever he can get it! He knows its FOOD VALUE and that it never fails to increase STAMINA nor to resist DAMP and COLD. Easily carried, easily made, suitable for all emergencies.

**"In Itself a Perfect Food."**

*Dr Andrew Wilson, F.R.S.E., &c.*

Fry's Vinello Chocolate is a ready made food-confection and takes up little room. No more acceptable offering can be sent our gallant sailors and soldiers.

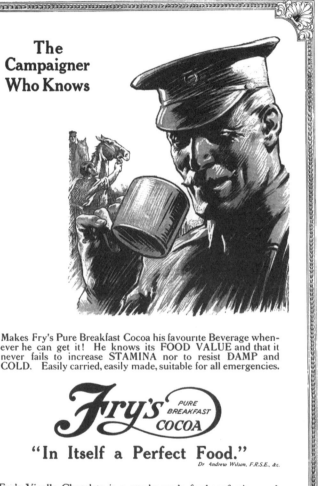

# 6

# MARCHING

## MARCHES.

### **24.** *General rules.*

1. Good marching depends largely on the attention paid to **march discipline**, under which head is included everything that affects the efficiency of man and horse during the march.

2. No compliments are to be paid during a march on service.

3. Space must be left on the right flank of a column (or as in Sec. **25**, 2), both when marching and when halted, for the passage of officers and of orderlies. Mounted officers, motor cars, and orderlies should avoid passing and re-passing infantry more than is absolutely necessary, and if it is necessary to do so should take advantage of halts for the purpose.

4. An officer, when available, will march in rear of each squadron, battery, company, or other unit, to see that no man quits the ranks without permission, that the sections, files, vehicles and animals keep properly closed up, and that the column does not unduly open out.

5. No trumpet or bugle call is allowed on the march, the column being directed by signal. A system of rapid communication will be established throughout every column.

Where roads cross one another or bifurcate, the general staff will arrange for orderlies to be placed to guide troops in the required direction, or the road not to be used may be blocked by some pre-arranged sign such as branches of trees, lines of stones, &c.

6. When there is much traffic which is liable to cause a block at any particular point, the general staff should arrange for an officer to regulate it.

### 25. *March formations and distances.*

1. On unenclosed ground it may sometimes be advisable to march on a broader front than the normal march formation.* One march formation should not be changed for another, unless the new formation can be maintained for a considerable distance.

2. In dusty and hot weather the column may with advantage be opened out on each side of the road, the centre of the road being kept clear. It may even be advisable to increase the distances and intervals between men, but this will only be done by order of the commander of the column.

3. To prevent minor checks in a column being felt throughout its length, the following distances will be maintained :—

| | |
|---|---|
| In rear of an infantry company ... ... ... | 10 yards. |
| ,, ,, squadron, battery, or other unit not specified here ... ... ... ... | 10 ,, |
| ,, ,, cavalry regiment, brigade R.A., or infantry battalion ... ... ... | 20 ,, |
| ,, ,, cavalry or infantry brigade ... ... | 30 ,, |
| ,, ,, a division ... | according to circumstances |

4. When marching by night (Sec. **132**, 8), and, by day, when an engagement is imminent, these distances may, by order of the commander of the column, be reduced, or even omitted altogether.

---

* The normal march formations on a road are—

| | |
|---|---|
| For cavalry and mounted rifles | Column of sections or of half sections, *i.e.*, 4 men or 2 men abreast. |
| ,, artillery ... ... | Column of route, *i.e.*, guns and wagons in single file. |
| ,, infantry ... ... | Column of fours. |

5. Staff officers must have, ready for reference, tables* showing the length of the body of troops with which they deal in column of route, time taken to pass a given point and to deploy, camping space required, &c.

### 26. *Pace.*

1. The rate of marching throughout a column should be uniform. The officer who sets the pace at the head of the column should bear in mind that an irregular pace tends to produce alternate checking and hurrying, which is most exhausting to the troops, especially to those in rear of the column.

2. If mounted troops are marching independently, the quicker the march is completed within certain limits the better. The pace should be regulated to suit the ground, the men will walk and lead frequently, particularly when ascending or descending steep hills.

3. If distances are lost on the march, stepping out, doubling, or trotting to regain them is forbidden, except by order of the commander of the unit. Infantry will be ordered to quicken its pace only if a defile is to be passed rapidly or some definite object is to be gained.

---

* It may be taken that all troops, mounted or dismounted, move to the starting point at the rate of 100 yards per minute, and that the following approximate space is occupied in column of route:—

| | | |
|---|---|---|
| Cavalry or mounted rifles in sections ... | 1 yard per horse in the ranks. | |
| ,, ,, ,, half sections | 2 yards ,, | ,, |
| Infantry in fours ... ... ... ... | 1 yard per 2 men | ,, |

Each 1 or 2 horse gun or vehicle takes 10 yards.
,, 4 ,, ,, ,, 15 ,,
,, 6 ,, ,, ,, 20 ,,
,, light tractor takes 5 yards.
,, lorry takes 6 yards.
,, 2 mule or pony vehicle takes 7 yards.
,, pack animal takes 4 yards.
,, camel takes 5 yards.

4. The length of an average march under normal conditions for a large column of all arms is fifteen miles a day, with a rest at least once a week; small commands of seasoned troops can cover twenty-five miles a day under favourable conditions.

5. Infantry should rarely be called upon to exceed the regulation rate of marching; such efforts usually fail in their object by exhausting the men. A forced march depends rather on the number of hours during which the troops are marching without long halts, than on the pace of marching. If troops are called upon to make a special effort, they should be made to understand that it is for a specific object.

* The average rate of marching for a large body of troops composed of all arms is $2\frac{1}{2}$ miles per hour including short halts. Rates of movement for small bodies of troops in the field are approximately as follows:—

| Arm. | Yards per minute. | Minutes required to traverse 1 mile. | Miles per hour, including short halts. |
|---|---|---|---|
| INFANTRY— | | | |
| Usual pace ... ... | 100 | 18 | 3 |
| MOUNTED TROOPS— | | | |
| Walk ... ... ... | 117 | 15 | $3\frac{1}{2}$ |
| Trot ... ... ... | 235 | 8 | 7 |
| Gallop ... ... ... | 440 | — | — |
| Trot and walk ... ... | — | — | 5 |

The following are the approximate rates of movement of Indian transport on a level road in single file:—

| | | |
|---|---|---|
| Pack mules or ponies ... ... | 250 | pass a given point in 10 minutes. |
| Camels ... ... ... ... | 100 | ,, ,, ,, |
| Pack bullocks ... ... ... | 160 | ,, ,, ,, |
| Army transport carts (mules or ponies) | 100 | ,, ,, ,, |
| Army transport carts (bullocks) | 60 | ,, ,, ,, |

Two mules, ponies, or bullocks to each cart. On rough, uneven, or hilly roads the above numbers should be halved.

Forced marching should be resorted to only when the expenditure of fighting power thereby entailed is justified by the object to be gained.

### 27. *Order of march.*

1. When there is no possibility of meeting an enemy, the order of march of the main body will depend chiefly upon the comfort of the troops. The comfort of the troops depends to a great extent upon convenience of supply, which is facilitated by preserving as long as possible the normal organization of units during the march.

2. When within reach of the enemy the order of march must be decided in accordance with the military situation. Units will then usually march in the order in which they would come into action, but artillery must be preceded by sufficient infantry to afford it protection. As a rule, part of the divisional artillery will follow the leading infantry brigade of the main body of its division.

Artillery brigade ammunition columns usually march in rear of the fighting troops of their own division or cavalry brigade, but it may be advisable to place one, or a portion of one, brigade ammunition column further forward in the order of march.

The position of air, signal, and bridging units in the column of march must depend on the requirements of the situation. The bridging train, if there is no chance of its being wanted for some time, may be one or more days' march in rear. In fixing its position the importance of keeping the roads in rear of the fighting troops clear must be considered.

Spare and led horses will march in rear of the first line transport of the units to which they belong.

Those portions of the engineer field companies, which are not with the advanced guard, will be accompanied by such technical vehicles only as are immediately required, and will usually march near the head of their own division. The remainder of their vehicles will be with such of the brigade ammunition columns as are marching in rear of the fighting troops.

Field ambulances* follow their own divisions unless otherwise ordered, and will usually march in rear of the brigade ammunition columns.

**28.** *Trains, supply columns, and flying corps transport.*

1. Horsed transport, called "trains," is allotted to divisions and to army troops for the carriage of the baggage, stores and supplies necessary for their subsistence. This transport mobilizes with the fighting troops and accompanies them to the area of concentration, where it is withdrawn and organized under the Director of Transport or his representative.

In the case of Royal Engineer units, trains are allotted for the transport of supplies only. The baggage of these units is carried in their technical vehicles.

The trains so formed are designated divisional trains and army troops trains.

They are organized in companies, which are subdivided into a baggage section and a supply section.

Commanders of units, other than Army Service Corps, detail one man per vehicle for escort and loading duties to accompany the transport, the party from each unit being under a non-commissioned officer or the oldest soldier. These parties should be changed as little as possible.

2. Generally speaking, when there is no likelihood of a collision with the enemy, the smaller the distance that intervenes between

* A field ambulance with its transport and equipment is divided into three sections, A, B, and C, each containing a bearer sub-division and a tent sub-division. When an engagement is imminent, a field ambulance or as many sections or parts of sections as may be necessary may be allotted to brigades and march with them. A section of a field ambulance or a part of a section, according to the size of the detachment, is normally sufficient for the service of a small temporary detachment such as an advanced guard. A cavalry field ambulance is similarly organized, but is more mobile, and is divided into two sections, A and B. A cavalry field ambulance may be allotted to a cavalry brigade, and its light ambulance wagons to detached regiments or smaller bodies of mounted troops.

the baggage sections of trains and the main body the better, as this transport is required as soon as the troops reach their destination. When there is a possibility that the enemy may be met, all other considerations must give way to the requirements of the military situation, and transport must not follow the main body so closely as to hamper its movements or those of neighbouring formations.

3. The transport of each brigade or of divisional troops marches in the same order within its train unit as the brigade, &c., which it serves.

4. The general system of forwarding supplies is described in detail in "Field Service Regulations," Part II. The supply sections of the trains are refilled by the supply columns (mechanical transport) which are lines of communication units. These supply columns proceed from rail head to rendezvous, which are normally fixed for the various divisions or other formations by general or army headquarters, though the power to fix rendezvous may be delegated to divisional commanders.

The divisional and other commanders are responsible that the columns containing supplies for their commands are met at their rendezvous and conducted to refilling points, which are normally fixed by them. At these refilling points the supplies are transferred to the supply sections of the train.

In the case of cavalry formations, which are not provided with trains, supply columns deliver direct to the troops.

5. When contact with the enemy is possible, the probable movements of the fighting troops must be considered in fixing the position of rendezvous and of refilling points, which should be arranged so as not to interfere with such movements. If the military situation makes it advisable, the position of refilling points as well as the rendezvous may be fixed by general or army headquarters.

6. If the supply sections of the trains have been refilled before the baggage sections march, both sections may march together; occasions will arise, however, when it is necessary to fix the

position of refilling points some distance in rear of the fighting troops, and in these circumstances the supply sections may have to march separately.

7. The maintenance of aircraft in the field demands a large number of transport vehicles, which require careful control by the staff of the headquarters* to which the squadrons or flights are attached.

8. Squadrons or flights employed with the cavalry on a special mission should be accompanied by all their transport if the situation permits.

9. Squadrons under general headquarters which are pushed forward to the protective troops, should be accompanied only by the first echelon and such portion of the second echelon as is absolutely necessary for their efficient maintenance, the remainder moving in rear of the trains.

10. During the forward movement the successive landing grounds of squadrons with army corps or divisions will be located in rear of the other arms, and the greater part of their transport will therefore follow in rear of the fighting troops. A few light cars from the first echelon will be sent forward at the earliest opportunity to the new landing ground. It will often be possible

---

* The transport of an aeroplane squadron is divided into two echelons.

*1st Echelon.*

1 light tender for the squadron commander.
For each flight.—2 motor bicycles.
2 light tenders.
2 heavy tenders.
Total for a squadron.—6 motor bicycles.
7 light tenders.
6 heavy tenders.

*2nd Echelon.*

3 repair lorries.
3 reserve equipment lorries, each with trailer.
3 shed lorries, each with trailer.
1 M.T. repair lorry.
1 M.T. reserve equipment lorry.

to get these cars past the troops during a long halt. The heavy tenders of the first echelon transport will move either between the supply and baggage sections of the divisional train or in rear of both. The second echelon of the transport will generally be brought forward to the landing ground as early as possible, but the necessity for leaving the roads free may make it necessary for this echelon to follow the divisional supply column as far as refilling points.

### 29. *Divisional ammunition columns.*

Divisional ammunition columns form part of the divisional artillery, and are therefore under the immediate orders of the divisional artillery commanders. Their position on the line of march is regulated by divisional headquarters in ordinary circumstances, but it may, if necessary, be fixed by army corps or general headquarters.

### 30. *Starting point.*

1. A point, termed the starting point, which the head of the main body is to pass at a certain time, is fixed in operation orders. If troops are not all quartered together, it may be necessary for the commander to fix more than one starting point, so as to enable subordinate commands to take their places in the column of march punctually without unnecessary fatigue to the troops, and without crossing the line of march of other commands. In the absence of such orders subordinate commands must arrange their own movements to the starting point. When commands are broken up for administration and discipline in quarters, the responsibility for the arrangements for the resumption of a march by the troops quartered in an area rests with the brigade area commander as far as the divisional starting point.

2. In fixing the starting point, care must be taken that each unit reaches it by moving forward in the direction of the march.

3. Should the march begin in the dark, the starting point will usually be marked by signalling lamps, or by fires, the method of

marking it being mentioned in the operation orders. If a force, which is scattered in quarters, is required to pass a common starting point in the dark, it will often be advisable to post a chain of men, at distances of about 20 yards, between the assembly grounds of brigades, &c., and the starting point, arrangements being made for collecting these men when they are no longer required.

4. During the movement to the starting point, troops with their first line transport have precedence on the road of all other transport, which should remain parked on its own ground till the fighting troops are clear, being then moved direct into its place in the column.

### 31. *Halts.*

1. On the HALT being signalled, everyone, when the force is not in contact with the enemy, will at once halt and fall out on the left side of the road. The signal for the halt will be given from the head of the main body. Commanders of protective troops will exercise their discretion as to halting at once, or moving forward to occupy a position which may be of more tactical advantage. The responsibility for protection during halts remains with the troops which have been protecting the march until they are relieved.

On the ADVANCE being signalled, troops will at once fall in and resume the march.

2. A short halt will be ordered soon after the column has started, in the case of both mounted and dismounted troops, subsequent halts being arranged at regular intervals at the discretion of the commander of the column, who should let commanders of units know how often they may expect halts and their duration. The notification of these arrangements is a matter of routine which should usually be arranged for in standing orders.

3. Halts are of most use when equipment can be removed to ease the men, teams unhooked, and horses unsaddled.

4. During hot weather, on long marches, or when the march is

begun at a very early hour, arrangements should be made for watering animals during the march. If a long halt is contemplated, a staff officer accompanied by an engineer and a medical officer, with sufficient police and orderlies, should be sent forward to select halting grounds near good water. He should arrange for the methodical distribution of the water supply, and take measures for its protection until the main body arrives.

### 32. *Military bridges, fords, drifts, &c.**

1. The responsibility for the construction of a bridge should be defined at the time when it is ordered to be built, and suitable provision for its safety and maintenance be made.

2. If a military bridge is to be passed, a river forded, or defile passed, a general staff officer or an officer detailed by the general staff will be posted on the approach to give commanders of units instructions on special points that are to be observed in crossing.

3. To see that distances are not unduly opened out, to prevent unnecessary delays, and to make such arrangements as may be necessary to prevent troops in rear being checked, an officer from each unit will remain on the near side of the bridge, drift, &c., until the whole of the unit has passed it.

4. When crossing a military bridge, infantry must break step. Files or sections must not be closed up.

5. If it be absolutely necessary to halt on a pontoon bridge, the wheels of guns and wagons must be halted as nearly as possible midway between two boats.

6. If a bridge sways so as to become very unsteady, the column must be halted till the swaying ceases.

7. All horses, other than spare horses, should be mounted when crossing a bridge. Spare horses should be led across by mounted men, no man leading more than one. The pace is never to be

---

* For further instructions regarding the passage of rivers, &c., *see* "Manual of Field Engineering."

faster than a walk. Drivers who have crossed the bridge are not to increase their pace for some distance after crossing.

8. The following depths are fordable :—

By infantry, 3 feet; by cavalry, 4 feet; by artillery, 2 feet 4 inches.

Fords with gravelly bottoms are best ; those with sandy bottoms are bad, as the sand gets stirred up, and the depth of water thus increases. Fords should be clearly marked by long pickets driven into the river bed above and below the ford, their heads being connected by a strong rope. It is well to mark the pickets in order that any rise of the water may be at once evident.

Rivers which are not fordable straight across may be found passable in a slanting direction between two bends.

### 33. *Rules for horse and pack transport on the march.*

1. Strict march discipline is quite as necessary with transport as with troops. Opening out must be constantly checked, and lost distances corrected as opportunity occurs. All transport, both when marching and when halted, must leave sufficient space on the right flank for the free passage of officers and orderlies. Pack animals should not be loaded until shortly before they are required to move off. Animals must on no account be allowed to drink when passing fords unless an organized halt has been arranged for this purpose, nor should drivers be allowed to halt without special permission.

2. With mixed transport, *e.g.*, carts, camels, mules, &c., if the situation admits of the column opening out, the fastest class of transport should start first; this course is, however, dangerous if the convoy is liable to be attacked, in which case no opening out should be permitted. Over-driving slow moving animals such as camels, to make them keep up with fast moving animals such as mules, is especially to be guarded against. In each class of transport the slowest-moving team or animal should lead.

3. All non-commissioned officers and men not belonging to the escort or to the transport *personnel*, who for any reason may accompany the transport, will march together by units and will be at the disposal of the commander of the escort or in his absence of the senior transport officer. All followers and non-combatants will be allotted a definite position, and must not be allowed to leave it.

4. When pack mules or camels are used, each driver must lead his own animals (usually three in number). The practice of tying animals in long strings is prohibited. On rough hill tracks mules go best if they are not tied together. In open country road space can be much economised by moving transport on a broad front, so long as recurring defiles do not entail frequent changes of front. It is especially convenient to clear a camping ground by moving off on a broad front. Ground scouts are often essential to a baggage column.

5. No one other than the driver is to ride on any cart, wagon, or transport animal without a written order from a transport officer.

6. Some empty wagons or spare animals should be in rear of the column to replace casualties. The proportion of spare transport animals normally allowed is supplied to relieve sick and broken-down transport and is not to be used to carry excess baggage.

7. Broken-down wagons, disabled animals, or thrown loads must at once be removed from the roadway, so that the transport in rear may not be checked.

8. When circumstances do not necessitate the train conforming to the march of other troops, a short halt should be made when the rear of the train is well clear of its starting point. Subsequent halts should be made at the discretion of the officer commanding train according to the nature and state of the roads, bearing in mind that halts are of most value when teams can be unhooked. Prolonged halts with the teams hooked in should at all times be avoided.

9. Transport arriving close to a village, bridge, or other defile at the end of a march should usually be encamped on the further

side. It is easier to pass such places whilst still in march formation than to do so, possibly in the dark, at the beginning of the next day's march. Local or tactical considerations may, however, affect this question.

10. Loading pack transport requires careful arrangement owing to the large number of men required. Under favourable circumstances four men can load 60 mules in an hour, if the loads are roped beforehand and laid out balanced in pairs so that the animals can walk between them to be loaded. Camels take perhaps four times as long to load. If therefore the animals are not to be loaded by the troops before starting (para. 1), a very strong baggage guard (experience has shown that 80 men per battalion is not excessive) must be left. The loading of pack supply columns is even more difficult to arrange, and it is often necessary to attach several days' supplies and its transport to each unit, so as to provide the necessary labour for loading.

11. Although in a mountainous country transport can, as a rule, move only in single file, advantage should be taken of the numerous checks that occur, to shorten the transport column by forming up as many animals as possible on every piece of flat ground by the side of the road. The necessity for this should be impressed on all ranks of the transport and baggage guard, as if it is thoroughly and systematically carried out, the rear-guard will be closer up to the main body, and the force as a whole more compact.

## MISCELLANEOUS.

To prevent *wet boots* from shrinking fill them with oats overnight; the oats will swell and keep the boots from shrinking.

If you have difficulty in pulling on a wet boot, light a piece of paper, drop it into the boot, and let it burn itself out. It will not hurt the wet boot, but will cause a film of steam inside, which will act as a lubricant.

The "*Rule of the Road*" in France, Belgium, and Germany is the opposite to that obtaining in England: *i.e.*, horsemen and vehicles and troops keep to the *Right* of the road, and pass others going in the same direction on the latter's *Left*.

A round of ammunition, or *3 pennies* or 5 halfpennies (French or English), weigh 1 ounce. A halfpenny is one inch in diameter.

## HOW TO PREVENT SORE FEET.

To prevent sore feet cleanliness and strict attention to the fitting of boots and socks are necessary. Before marching the feet should be washed with soap and water and carefully dried. The inside of the socks should be well rubbed with soft or yellow soap. After the march the feet must be again washed and clean dry socks put on. Soaking the feet in salt or alum and water hardens the skin. The nails should be cut straight across and not too close. A blister will probably be occasioned by an unevenness or hole in the sock, or an unevenness in the lining of the boot; the cause, therefore, should be ascertained and removed. The edge of a blister should be pricked with a needle and the fluid drained away by gently pressing the blister; a small pad of cotton wool or soft rag should be applied, and kept in place by a small piece of sticking plaster. Men are cautioned against getting boots too small for them.

## III.

### *Air,* "John Peel."

1. D'ye ken John French, with his khaki suit,
His belt and his gaiters, and stout brown boot,
Along with his guns, and his horse, and his foot,
On the road to Berlin in the morning?

*Chorus—*
Yes, we ken John French, and old Joffre too,
And all his men to the Tricolor true,
And Belgians and Russians, a jolly good few,
On the road to Berlin in the morning.

2. The Prussian Kaiser must be made to kneel,
The Prussian Eagle must be made to feel
The force of the bullet and the good cold steel,
On the road to Berlin in the morning.

*Chorus—*
For we ken John French, and old Joffre too,
And all his men to the Tricolor true,
And Belgians and Russians, a jolly good few,
On the road to Berlin in the morning.

3. For the mothers they slew, and the kids as well,
And for sundry things it's not fit to tell,
We've got to catch 'em and to give 'em hell,
On the road to Berlin in the morning.

*Chorus—*
For we ken John French, and old Joffre too,
And all his men to the Tricolor true,
And Belgians and Russians, a jolly good few,
On the road to Berlin in the morning.

III. Air: "JOHN PEEL."
Doh is D.
1. D' ye ken John French, with his kha - ki suit, His
belt and his gai - ters, and stout brown boot, A -
- long with his guns, and his horse, and his foot, On the
road to Ber - lin in the morn - ing?
CHORUS.
Yes, we ken John French, and old Jof - fre, too, And
all his men to the Tri - col-our true; And
Bel - gians and Rus-sians, a jol - ly good few, On the
road to Ber - lin in the morn - ing!

## VI.

### *Air,* " Tramp, Tramp, Tramp."

1. In the midst of foreign wars,
Half-asleep beneath the stars,
We think of happy homes so far away ;
We think of those we love,
And we pray to God above,
Once more to let us see them and be gay.

*Chorus—*
Tramp, tramp, tramp, the boys are marching ;
Cheer up, comrades, we will come.
And beneath the Union Jack
We will drive the Germans back,
For the safety of our own belovèd home.

2. In the battle front we stand,
And we strike for Fatherland,
And we only think of getting at the foe,
And we do not make a fuss,
Though we know it's him or us,
But we fancy that it's him that's got to go.

*Chorus—*
Tramp, tramp, tramp, the boys are marching ;
Cheer up, comrades, we will come.
And beneath the Union Jack
We will drive the Germans back,
For the safety of our own belovèd home.

3. And we've got a thought beside,
Of the friends who fought and died,
The best of pals that ever held a gun ;
And there comes a feeling strong,
That it won't be very long
Till we get the *bally* Germans on the run.

*Chorus—*
Tramp, tramp, tramp, the boys are marching ;
Cheer up, comrades, we will come.
And beneath the Union Jack
We will drive the Germans back,
For the safety of our own belovèd home.

VI. AIR: "TRAMP, TRAMP, TRAMP."
Doh is B♭.
1. In the midst of foreign wars, Half a-sleep beneath the stars, We
think of hap-py homes so far a-way; We
think of those we love, And we pray to God a-bove, Once
more to let us see them and be gay.
CHORUS.
Tramp, tramp, tramp, the boys are march - ing—
Cheer up, comrades, we will come, And be-
-neath the Union Jack We will drive the Germans back, For the
safe-ty of our own be-lov-ed home.

## 13.

### THE BRITISH GRENADIERS.

Some talk of Alexander,
And some of Hercules,
Of Hector and Lysander,
And such great names as these;
But of all the world's great heroes
There's none that can compare,
With a tow row row row row row,
With the British Grenadiers.

Whene'er we are commanded
To storm the palisades,
Our leaders march with fusees,
And we with hand-grenades;
We throw them from the glacis
About the enemies' ears,
Sing tow row row row row row,
The British Grenadiers.

And when the siege is over,
We to the town repair,
The townsmen cry hurrah, boys,
Here comes a Grenadier:
Here come the Grenadiers, my boys,
Who know no doubts or fears,
Then sing tow row row row row row,
The British Grenadiers.

Then let us fill a bumper,
And drink a health to those
Who carry caps and pouches,
And wear the loupéd clothes.
May they and their commanders
Live happy all their years,
With a tow row row row row row
For the British Grenadiers.

# 7

# COMMUNICATION

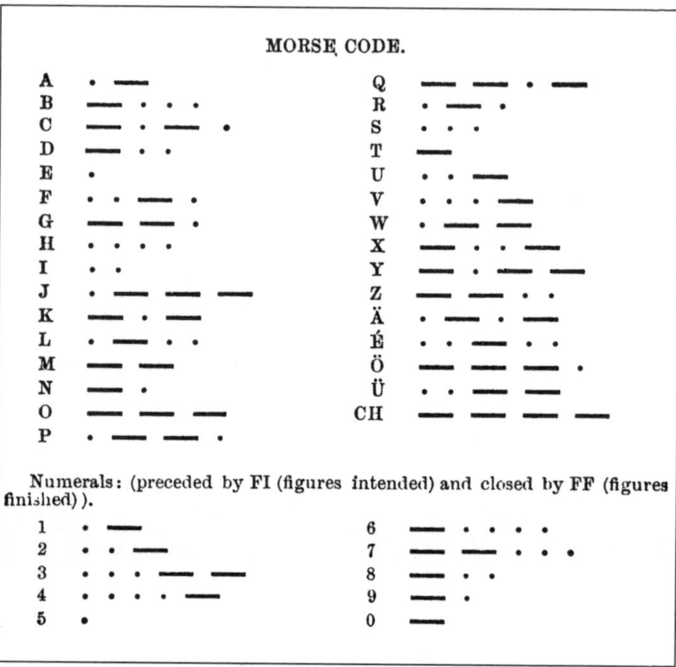
MORSE CODE.
A · —
B — · · ·
C — · — ·
D — · ·
E ·
F · · — ·
G — — ·
H · · · ·
I · ·
J · — — —
K — · —
L · — · ·
M — —
N — ·
O — — —
P · — — ·
Q — — · —
R · — ·
S · · ·
T —
U · · —
V · · · —
W · — —
X — · · —
Y — · — —
Z — — · ·
Ä · — · —
É · · — · ·
Ö — — — ·
Ü · · — —
CH — — — —
Numerals: (preceded by FI (figures intended) and closed by FF (figures finished)).
1 · —
2 · · —
3 · · · — —
4 · · · · —
5 ·
6 — · · · ·
7 — — · · ·
8 — · ·
9 — ·
0 —

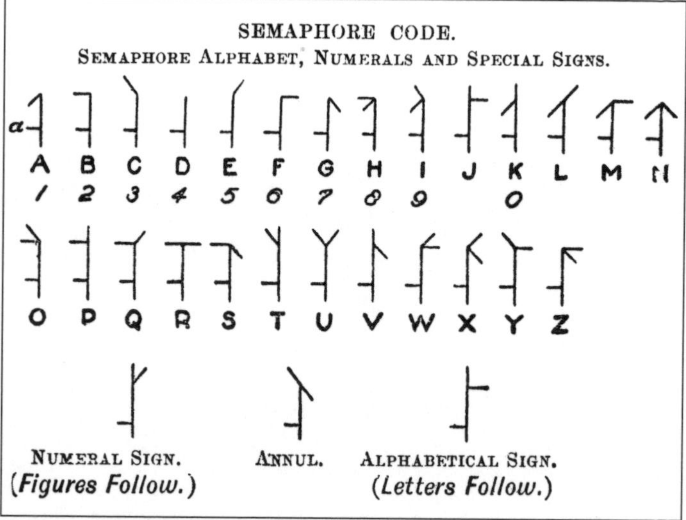
SEMAPHORE CODE.
SEMAPHORE ALPHABET, NUMERALS AND SPECIAL SIGNS.
a
A B C D E F G H I J K L M N
1 2 3 4 5 6 7 8 9 0
O P Q R S T U V W X Y Z
NUMERAL SIGN. (Figures Follow.)
ANNUL.
ALPHABETICAL SIGN. (Letters Follow.)

*Semaphore Code*—continued.

The small arm at *a* is called the "Indicator," and shows the side from which the Alphabet or signs commence; the signaller, when working a fixed semaphore, is sometimes not visible, and the indicator is necessary because his back may be toward the reader. It also often happens on board ship that a semaphore signal is being read from both sides at the same time, and unless the indicator were used the reverse letters might be read, *e.g.*, K for V.

The above figures also represent the semaphore-flagger as *facing* the reader.

## Intercommunication between Army and Navy.

*Special signals for opening communication.*—Two special signals are established for distinguishing intercommunication between the two services when wishing to call one another up, viz.:—

(*a*) *By day.*—The "Naval and Military Pendant," which is white with 2 black crosses. This is always to be used by H.M. ships wishing to communicate with a shore station, or by a shore station equipped with a flagstaff and possessing this pendant wishing to attract the attention of one of H.M. ships.

The above must not be confused with the "Negative Flag," sometimes used by H,M. ships between themselves. The latter is a white square flag with five black crosses on it.

(*b*) *By night or by day.*—The "Military Sign," which is the letter X made either by Morse or Semaphore. This sign is invariably to be used at night, and during daylight by stations which have no flagstaff or military pendant available.

## CIPHERS.

For deciphering ciphers of which the key word is unknown, the following may be of assistance, as giving the comparative frequency in different languages of different letters.

In all 3 languages E is of the greatest frequency, occurring in English about 12 times, in French 18 times, and in German 14 times, in 100 letters.

Other letters, in their order of frequent occurrence, are:—

| | |
|---|---|
| English ... ... ... ... | T A O N I S R H. |
| French ... ... ... ... | S A N T I R U L. |
| German ... ... ... ... | N I R S T U D A. |

# FIELD TELEPHONES.

The present war has proved how necessary it is for troops of all arms to be equipped with a supply of field telephones for communication when under cover, by having observers suitably placed for observing artillery fire, and for the passing of orders in trenches.

A field telephone is of little value unless the operator is properly trained to both the correct way of talking on it, or failing that (due to cable trouble or noise of artillery fire) in sending the message by Morse on the buzzer. He should also be trained in the adjustments and minor repairs to his instrument, about which I propose later to give a few details.

The operator should have an elementary knowledge of electricity to enable him to understand the construction and action of the following:—

(*a*) The dry cell.
(*b*) Construction and action of buzzer magnet.
(*c*) Induction coil.
(*d*) Microphone (Capsule type).
(*e*) Receiver.

An operator without electrical knowledge should be taught—(*a*) the rough tests of the instrument; (*b*) the care of the battery and how to connect it up; (*c*) the object of the buzzer adjusting screw and how to adjust it; (*d*) the correct way to talk a message.

It will be seen from the sketch (see Fig.) that the battery sends a current through the buzzer magnet coils down the armature and through the adjusting screw. If the buzzer fails to work on pressing the key it is usually either due to a weak battery, want of adjustment to the screw, or a wire disconnected somewhere.

If these points are understood a man without electrical knowledge should be able to put the instrument in order unassisted.

Several recent types of field telephones have a combined induction coil and buzzer, the iron

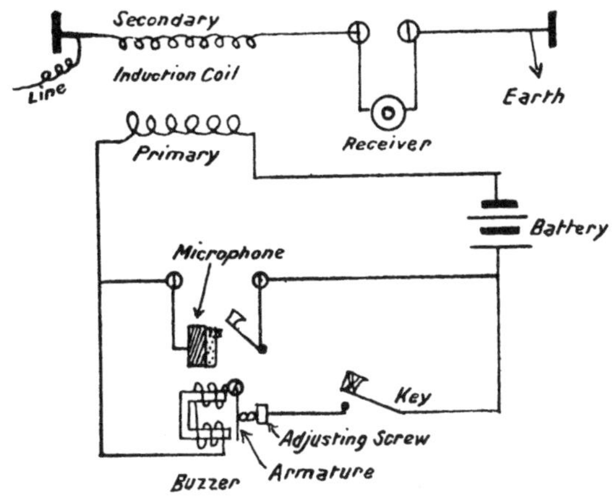


Field Telephone Circuits.

core of which, being energised by the primary coil, is made to attract the armature.

**Faults that occur in a field telephone and how to overcome them** :—

| Fault. | Remedy. |
|---|---|
| **Buzzer fails to act.** | |
| Adjusting screw. | It should be turned back and then forward until it just touches the armature. |
| Weak battery. | Test cells with a cell tester, and replace the weak ones. |
| Battery wire disconnected. | Examine battery connections and see that the wire joining the cells in series is connected. |

| Fault. | Remedy. |
|---|---|
| **Buzz not heard in receiver with line terminals short circuited.** | |
| Break in receiver cord. | Moisten two fingers (on one hand) and place on receiver cord terminals. Press key. If slight shock is felt the cord is broken. Repair or replace it. |
| **No sounds heard in receiver when blowing into the microphone, with line terminals short circuited.** | |
| Break in microphone cord. | Make and break with a coin between the terminals that cord is connected to. If this is heard it is either a break in the cord or a fault in the microphone capsule itself. Repair or replace the former, if the latter replace it. |

**Cable.**—The cable for field telephone work is usually made of a few strands of steel wire insulated, or a single strand enamelled wire. If the covering of the wire is removed at any point it should be re-covered by a layer of rubber tape. If cut, bare the ends, tie together, and lap with tape. As a temporary measure, a piece of rubber tubing slipped over the joint is a good substitute for tape. The cable should occasionally be overhauled when not in use, as it saves time and trouble after laying it out.

**Transmission of Messages.**—If possible, always talk a message. Should trouble be experienced in getting a word or words through, it is quicker to send it by Morse on the buzzer.

**Talking a Message.** — The sending operator should call out two or three words at a time slowly and clearly. The receiving operator should, as he writes each word, repeat it, as this lets the sending operator know when to go on. Figures should be sent thus :—9006 as, figures "nine double O six." When finished, sending operator says, "Message ends." Receiving operator checks back message slowly. Sending operator will correct mistakes if any; otherwise say "Correct."

Practice in sending messages by Morse on the buzzer should be freely indulged in, as it very frequently happens that, owing to noise or line faults, talking is either indistinct or impossible.

After you have once established communication, never leave your telephone without informing the distant operator that you are going to do so, and how long you are going to be away. If possible, find a substitute.

The telephone should have a head receiver, which should never be removed during work.

If, after communication has been established, you fail to get a reply from the distant station, send out your lineman to examine the wire. He should take a telephone with him to tap in (using a safety pin to get connection), and call the base operator to see if he has passed the fault or not.

A lineman should always be ready at each end of the line, and if they both leave when a breakdown occurs, they will avoid the trouble that is often experienced by one man having to go all along the wire, instead of half-way.

E. J. STEVENS.

## 101. Orders.

𝅗𝅥 = 76.
Come for Or - ders, come for Or - ders;

know the Corps is wait - ing for the Or - ders of

## 102. Orderly Room.

♩ = 108.
Now it's all Non-Coms who are on du

Col - 'nel's in his chair— you bet he won't spare

## 103. Post Call.

♩. = 104.
There goes the Call for let -

be sharp; hur - ry up! Come for Or - ders: You

lay— So come, let 'em have the news!

3
And Of - fi - cers an - swer this Call!

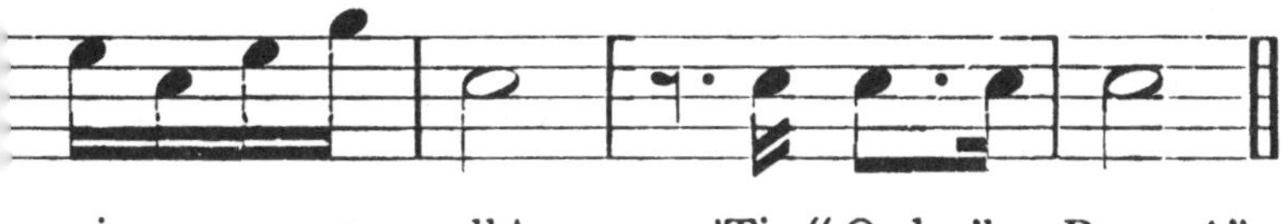
pri-son-ers at all! 'Tis "Ord - 'ly Room!"

La - test from "Home, Sweet Home!"

## 106. Fall in.

## 107. Dismiss, or No Parade.

Oh! there's no p'rade to-day ; Oh! there's no p'rade to-

ll in now, the short and the tall!
you stand up smart at the call!

t's jol - ly sel-dom that we get The chance to stay a - way.

## ade or Rides.

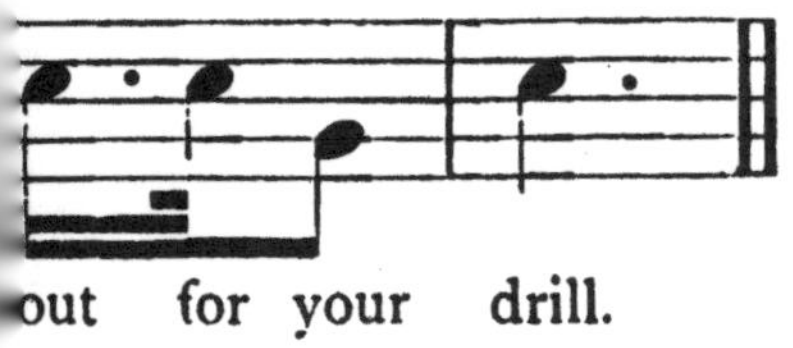
out for your drill.

## 114. Parade for Guard.

♩ = 108.

Come and do your guard, my boys! Come and do your

## 115. Fatigue.

I call'd them, I call'd them; they wouldn't come, they

## 116. Defaulters.

Now throw all your cleaning traps down on y

## 117. Sick.

𝅗𝅥 = 76.

Come the sick, come the lame, All cures

You've had fourteen nights in bed, So it won't be hard.

't come: I call'd them, I call'd them, they wouldn't come at all!

ts, And an - swer De - faul-ters, my boys.

3
ills we've got, To free Tom-my from pain.

## 122. Fire Alarm.

𝅗𝅥 = 108.
There's a fire! There's
Run and get the en - gine boys, and

## 123. Officers Dress for Dinner.

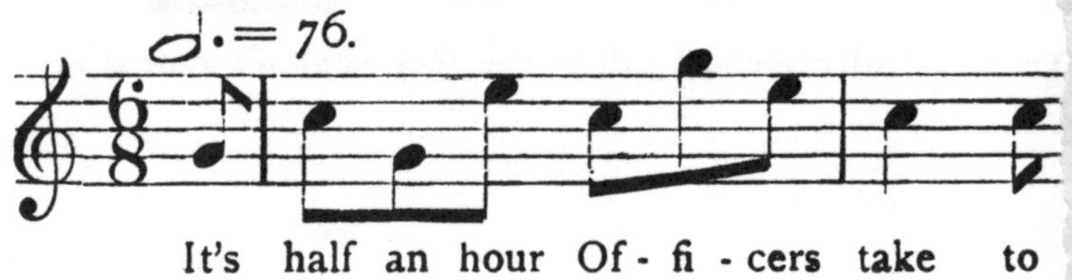
𝅗𝅥. = 76.
It's half an hour Of - fi - cers take to

## 124. Officers' Dinner.

𝅗𝅥. = 76.
Oh! what a time those Of - fi -
din - ner!...... Just give me theirs an

fire ! ! There's a fire ! ! !
he beg - gar out.

-Their din - ner must be jol - ly fine !

have— I'd like to have their
t them have mine : I bet they'll get much

## 127. Men's Meal (2nd Call).

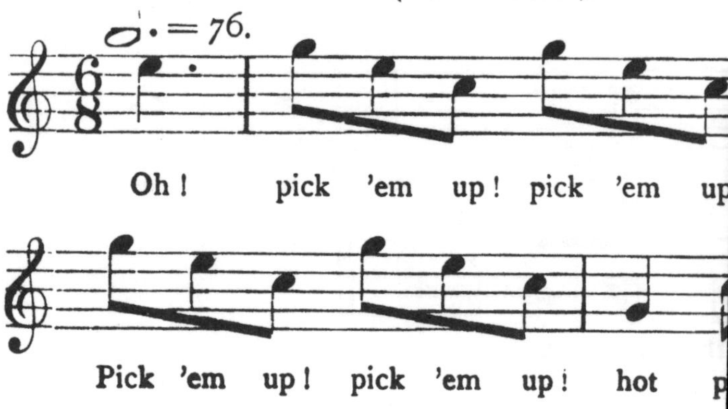


## 128. Salute for the Guard. (To be

## 129. The Reveille.

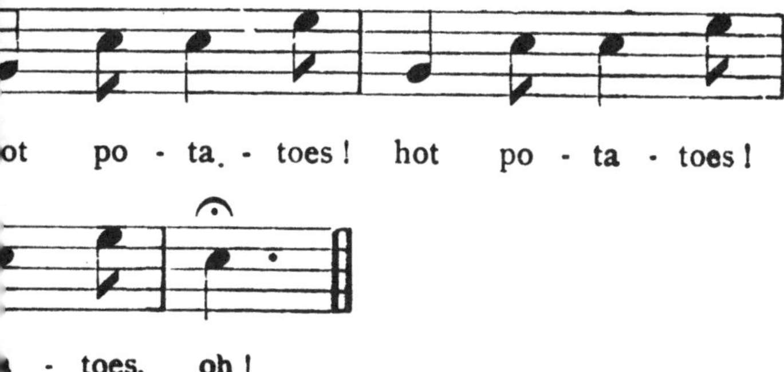
ot po - ta. - toes! hot po - ta - toes!
- toes, oh!

all occasions when Bugles are required to sound a salute.)

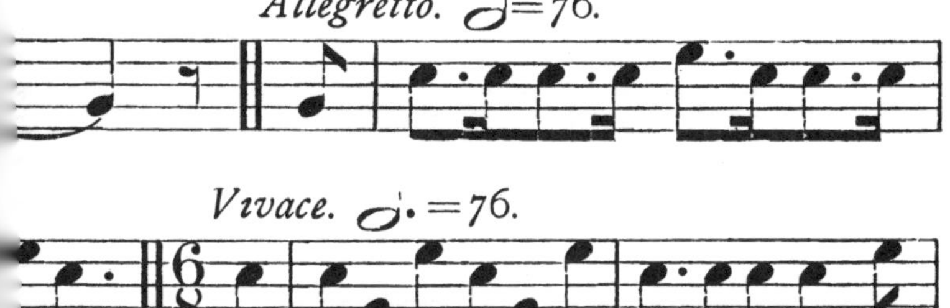
Allegretto. =76.
Vivace. =76.

**The Reveille**—*Continued.*

*Moderato.* ♩=108.

*Presto.* ♩=132.

## 133. Tattoo (Last Post).

Segue.

# 8

# TRENCH CONSTRUCTION

## 21. DEFENCE OF LOCALITIES, &c.

1. Localities of tactical importance may be commanding features of the ground, groups of substantial buildings and enclosures, or wooded knolls giving cover from view and a good field of fire to front and flanks.

2. Each locality should be capable of all-round defence, and each should be able to sweep with fire a large proportion of the ground lying between it and those on either side.

3. The principal defences will, as a rule, consist of fire trenches, hedges, and walls.

4. *Fire trenches* may be disposed in irregular lines or in groups with intervals, according to the character of the ground.

In selecting the sites for fire trenches, the following points require attention :—

(*a*) Good field of fire. Most important within 400 yards of the trench. Range marks, if possible, to be added.
(*b*) Concealment and invisibility. Obtained by adapting trenches to form of the ground, keeping parapets low, and by use of natural or artificial cover.
(*c*) Parapet should be bullet-proof.
(*d*) Head cover, which must be inconspicuous, should be provided, if possible.
(*e*) Trenches should be traversed or recessed.
(*f*) Cover for supports near at hand.
(*g*) Trenches should have steep interior slope, be wide enough to allow men to pass, and drainage should be provided. (For types *see* Plates 11 and 12.)

5. *Walls* can be notched or loopholed. The latter give the best cover, but should not be closer than 3 feet from centre to centre. Dummy loopholes should be added. If firing over the tops of walls is to be employed they should be covered with sods, turf, &c.

6. *Hedges* may be used as screens, or revetments to support the earth of a parapet. They must be thick enough to prevent the earth showing through. Work should be concentrated at first only at the points to be occupied by each man.

7. *Overhead cover* to keep out splinters of shell, &c., should consist of 9 to 12 inches of earth or 3 inches of shingle supported on brushwood, boards, corrugated iron, &c.

8. *Protected look-outs* will be needed for commanders, &c. A type is shown on Plate 11. This is also suitable for a sentry group in the outpost line.

9. *Roads* of a temporary nature are usually required :—

(*a*) In connection with a defensive position to enable troops or guns to be readily moved from one portion to another.
(*b*) For movement across country devoid of suitable tracks.

Within a position, troops and messengers should be guided to their destination by signposts, by " blazing " trees or other means.

10. A roadway 10 feet wide (8 feet minimum) will take a single line of wagons* passing in one direction, or infantry in fours ; 12 feet is better for allowing horsemen to pass without difficulty : for each additional line of vehicles 8 feet should be added to the width of the road. A width of 6 feet is sufficient for infantry in file or pack animals moving in one direction.

Gaps in walls, hedges, &c., forming road boundaries should be made at least 15 feet wide if intended for wheeled traffic.

11. The gradient for a short distance, such as a ramp leading on to a bridge, may be one-third or even one-half for infantry and one-seventh for

---

* The width over all service vehicles varies from 6 feet (Telegraph Cable Cart, Mk. II) to 7 feet (Ambulance Wagon, Mk. VI), and 2 wheel tracks, each 1 foot wide, spaced at 5 feet apart between inside edges, will accommodate all service vehicles.

## PLATE XI.

## COVER FOR SENTRY GROUP.
(Suitable for a Look-out Post).

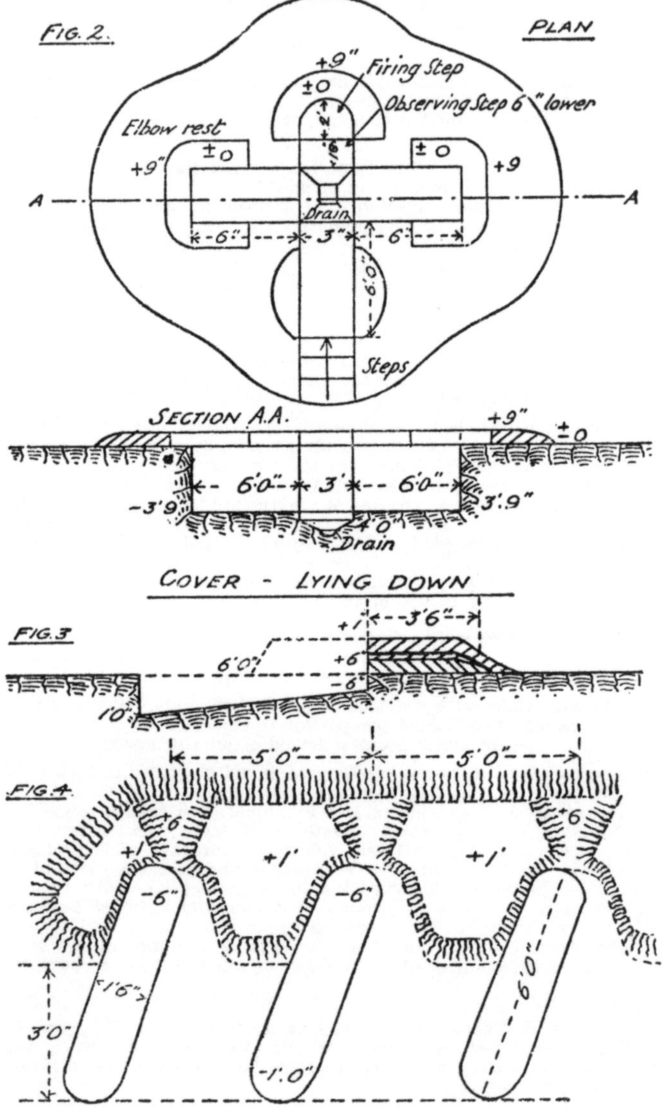

PLATE XII.

FIRE TRENCHES.

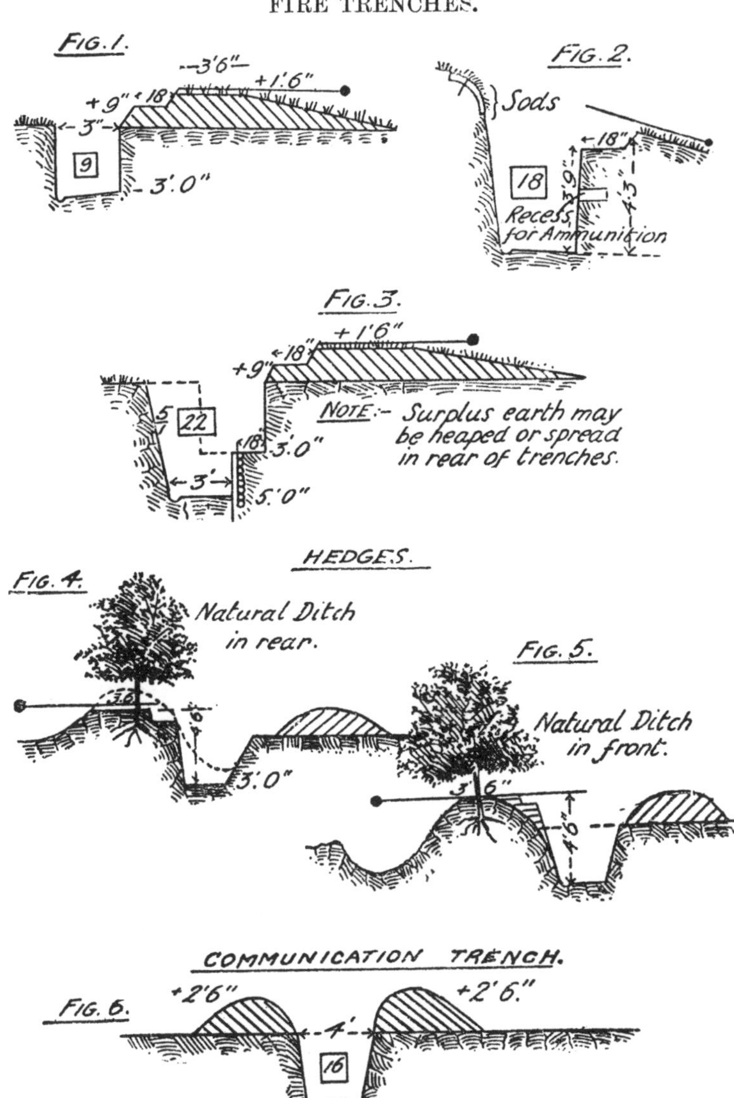


*To follow Plate XI.*

artillery, provided it is straight; but for animals or wheeled traffic slopes steeper than one-tenth are inconvenient, and if an incline is a long one its slope should be at least one-twentieth.

Traction engines can draw their own weight up one-tenth, twice their weight up one-twentieth, three times their weight on the level or up slopes not exceeding one-thirty-third.

12. When a road has to be constructed, the centre line should be marked by pickets, or the margins by *spitlocking*, and some kind of pathway cleared. The more difficult portions *must* be dealt with first, and the whole road rendered passable by artillery before any portion is still further improved.

13. When ascending a hill by means of zig-zags the road should be made as level as possible at each angle, and half as wide again as in the straight portions. The road should be prolonged uphill about 12 yards beyond each turn to enable teams to pull straight until the vehicle reaches the level turn. Short zig-zags should be avoided, and no curves should be sharper than with a radius of 60 feet for traffic of all arms to meet and pass without producing a deadlock.

14. The best foundation for a temporary road over boggy ground is one or more layers of fascines or hurdles; the top row must lie across the direction of the traffic, touching one another. When time is short or suitable material is not at hand, much can be done by throwing down brushwoods, heather, or even straw or grass laid across the road. It is quite useless to place stones or earth in small quantities upon a yielding foundation.

15. Where timber is available and heavy traffic is expected, a "corduroy" road may be made by felling trees, and laying them across the road at right angles to its direction, ribands being spiked to them at either end or the logs may be held together by interlacing with rope or wire.

The interstices between fascines, brushwood, logs, &c., may be filled with small stones and earth to make a better surface.

### VILLAGES.

16. For the defence of a village, a definite garrison should be detailed under the command of a selected officer. The latter will be responsible for selecting the main and any interior lines of defence, for dividing the village into sub-sections, for allotting to each a proportion of the garrison, for arranging for a central hospital for wounded men, and for notifying the position of his headquarters. A general reserve should be retained to deliver local counter-attacks.

17. Each subordinate commander should consider the preparations for the defence of his sub-section in the following order:—

- (*a*) Improvement of the field of fire.
- (*b*) Provision of cover, much of which may be done concurrently with (*a*).
- (*c*) Provision and improvement of communications.
- (*d*) Provision of obstacles and barricades.
- (*e*) Arrangements for extinguishing fires.
- (*f*) Ammunition supply.
- (*g*) Food and water.
- (*h*) Removal of sick and wounded.
- (*j*) Retrenchment.

18. At first the firing line should usually be placed in front of any buildings to prevent casualties from shells which burst against their walls.

### POSTS.

19. For the defence of a post the following are points to remember:—

- (*a*) Organization of inner and outer defences.
- (*b*) Defenders should be quartered close to the positions they have to man.
- (*c*) Arrangements for storage of ammunition, water and supplies.
- (*d*) Provision of strong obstacles.
- (*e*) Adequate cover with a clear field of fire.
- (*f*) Provision of automatic alarms, if possible.
- (*g*) Good communications, including telephones, telegraphs, and signalling.

### Buildings.

20. For the defence of a building the following points require attention :—

(*a*) Bullet-proof barricades to doors and windows. The means of exit, not necessarily on the ground floor, must be dealt with in a special way. It is easier to make loopholes in the barricades rather than to attempt to loophole the walls.

(*b*) Arrangements for ventilation, for the storage of ammunition, provisions and water, for a hospital and for latrines.

(*c*) Arrangements for extinguishing fires.

(*d*) Destruction of any outlying buildings which are not to be occupied, bearing in mind the importance of leaving no adjacent cover where an enemy might collect for assault.

21. If the building is large and strongly built, and it is intended to make an obstinate defence, arrangements must be made for interior defence by loopholing partition walls and upper floors made bullet-proof and strengthened if necessary to sustain the extra weight. Material with which to improvise additional cover or movable barricades to cover the retreat from one part of the building to the other, or from one building to another, must also be provided.

### Field Redoubts.

22. Field redoubts are works entirely enclosed by defensible parapets which give all-round rifle fire, and may be of any command.

Under ordinary conditions redoubts in defensive positions must not be designed or sited in such a way that they can be recognized as such by the enemy. This will prevent their employment in the main zone of defence as a general rule.

Their principal use will be on the lines of communication, for isolated posts and sometimes as supporting points in rear of a defended position.

23. Rules for trenches apply to redoubts, but the following additional points are important :—

(*a*) Plan or trace of a redoubt depends on : (*a*) Fire effect required from it ; (*b*) Configuration of the ground ; (*c*) Proposed garrison.

(*b*) If possible interior not to be seen from ground which may be occupied by enemy. If the inside is exposed the garrison must burrow.

(*c*) Good splinter-proof cover.

(*d*) Good obstacles.

(*e*) No dead angles.

(*f*) Faces long enough to give an effective fire

(*g*) Proportion of all defenders to size of work from 1 to 1½ men per yard of parapet.

(*h*) Overhead cover.

(*j*) Latrines and cooking places.

(*k*) Provide for water supply.

### Cover for Guns.

24. Plate 13 shows types of cover for guns.

### Woods.

25. The two attributes common to most woods are the obstruction they offer to the passage of troops, and the concealment they provide.

Special precautions are necessary for the defence of woods which run down from a position towards the enemy, since they make co-operation between the artillery and infantry of the defence almost impossible and afford the enemy a covered line of approach.

In the case of most woods the improvement of communications is one of the first considerations.

26. The front edge of a wood often has a boundary capable of being quickly made into a good fire position, but usually offers a good mark for artillery fire ; for this reason it may be desirable to place the firing line some 200 yards in advance, this being about the maximum distance short of the wood at which shrapnel should be burst, in order to be effective.

## Plate XIII.

*Fig.* 1.—Gun Pit for Shielded Gun.

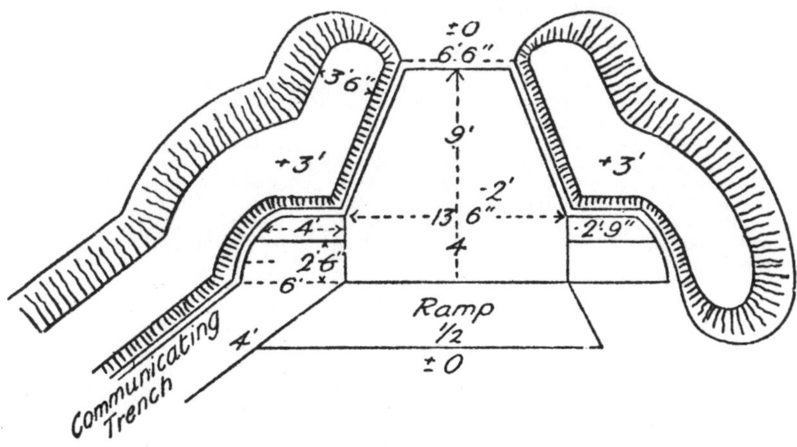


*Fig.* 2.—Gun Epaulment for Shielded Gun.

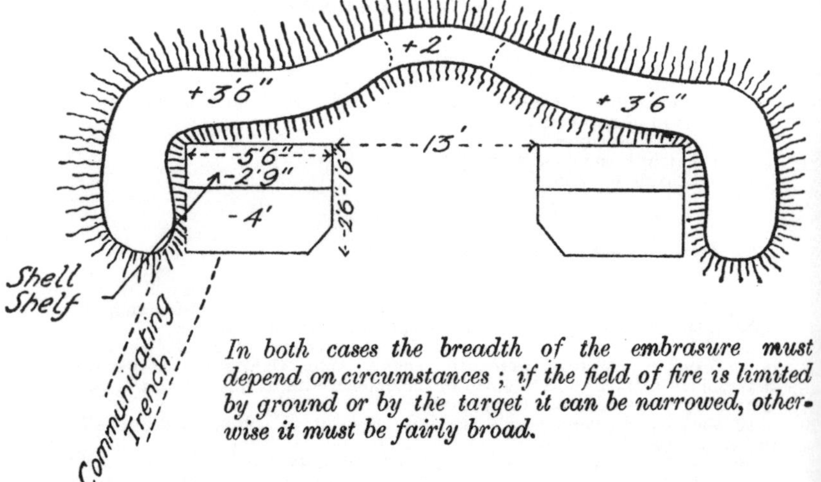


*In both cases the breadth of the embrasure must depend on circumstances; if the field of fire is limited by ground or by the target it can be narrowed, otherwise it must be fairly broad.*

If by clearing the undergrowth a good field of fire can be obtained between the tree trunks, the firing line may sometimes be placed with advantage 25 to 50 yards within the wood.

Where roads, rides or clearings exist in a wood, the rear edge may be organized as a second line of defence.

27. If defences in rear of a wood are more convenient than in front, the best arrangement will be to straighten and entangle the flanks and rear edge and take up an enfilading position some distance behind. Communications throughout the wood should be blocked.

## 22. OBSTACLES.

1. OBSTACLES ARE USED TO OBTAIN A DEFINITE CONTROL, BOTH AS REGARDS DIRECTION AND SPEED, OVER THE PROGRESS OF TROOPS ADVANCING TO THE ATTACK. THEIR CHIEF VALUE LIES IN THEIR POWER TO DEFLECT THE ATTACKING TROOPS INTO AREAS MOST FAVOURABLE FOR THEIR DESTRUCTION BY THE DEFENDERS. With this object in view they should be arranged: (*a*) to break up the unity of action and cohesion of the attacking troops, (*b*) to deflect the parties thus isolated into the best swept fields of fire, and (*c*) to arrest them under the close fire of the defenders. They are specially useful against night attacks.

2. They should fulfil the following conditions:—

(*a*) They should be under the close rifle of the defender, the outer edge not more than about 100 yards from the parapet. For small posts or redoubts they should be *quite close*, so that they may be effectively defended at night; but, if they are much less than the distance given above, it will be possible to throw hand grenades into the work. They should be as wide as time and material will allow, should afford the enemy no cover, and should be sheltered from his artillery fire. Their actual position will generally be determined by placing them where they can be covered by the most effective fire of the defenders.

(*b*) They should be difficult to remove or surmount, and will be most effective if special appliances (not usually carried by troops) are required for their removal. Special attention should be paid to the security of their anchorages.

(*c*) They should, if possible, be so placed that their exact position and nature are unknown to the attacking force. With this object their sites may be sunk. Conspicuously placed obstacles may betray the existence of an otherwise well concealed position.

(*d*) They should be arranged so as not to impede counter-attacks.

(*e*) They should not be constructed without authority from the commander of the section of the defence.

(*f*) They need not be continuous, but may be constructed in sections. Occasional gaps in the line will often lead the attackers to crowd in towards them. Such passages may be provided with land mines and must be covered by gun and rifle fire. Roads passing through obstacles, and occasionally required for use by the defence, should be closed by portable obstacles, such as chevaux de frise, when not required for traffic.

3. The greatest length of obstacle which can be controlled by one man on a stormy and dark night is about 35 yards on either side. Where the total length of obstacle exceeds 70 yards, additional sentries, systematic patrolling, or efficient mechanical alarm signals will be necessary.

## 23. WORKING PARTIES AND THEIR TASKS.

1. With full-sized tools the average soldier should excavate in ordinary soil the following volumes in each hour:—

| | |
|---|---|
| 1st hour .. .. .. .. .. .. .. | 30 cubic feet. |
| 2nd „ .. .. .. .. .. .. .. | 25 „ |
| 3rd „ .. .. .. .. .. .. .. | 15 „ |
| 4th „ and after, up to 8 hours .. .. .. | 10 „ |

or 80 cubic feet in a 4-hour relief.

If the soil is very easy these rates may be increased, and *vice versa*; and if 2 men are detailed to each set of tools these rates may be multiplied by $\frac{4}{3}$.

These rates hold good for a maximum horizontal throw of 12 feet, combined with a lift out of a trench 4 feet deep.

2. The proportion of picks to shovels will be decided according to the nature of the soil. In ordinary soil the entrenching implement is almost equal to a pick. In moderately hard ground a good proportion of tools (excluding the entrenching implements) is 110 shovels, 55 picks with 60 helves, and 10 crowbars per 100 men, working continuous reliefs up to a total of 40 hours. This proportion gives sufficient spare to enable defective tools to be rejected.

3. IN THE CASE OF FIRE TRENCHES ALL QUESTIONS OF MECHANICAL SPACING AND DISTRIBUTION MUST GIVE WAY TO THE SELECTION, ON THE GROUND, OF THE BEST FIRING POINT FOR EACH AVAILABLE RIFLE.

4. For continuous trenchwork the normal distance apart at which men are spaced for work is two paces (5 feet).

5. The following form may be useful to facilitate *rapid commencement of work* and to ensure that *men and tools are employed in the most advantageous manner*.

The commander of the unit concerned (in this example a battalion) details his men and tools to the works in their respective order of importance, as shown in Cols. 1, 2, 3, 4 and 5. Should the tools with the unit not be sufficient, the commander would then apply to his superior for the remainder.

The latter would then fill in Col. 6, showing whence the balance of tools required was to be obtained.

EXAMPLE OF WORKING PARTY TABLE.

WATLING RIDGE POSITION, NO. 2 SECTION (13TH INFANTRY BRIGADE).
1ST SCOTS FUSILIERS.

| 1 | 2 | | 3 | 4 | 5 | 6 |
|---|---|---|---|---|---|---|
| Task. (1″ Map Sheet 384.) | Men. | | Tools required. | Tools with unit. | Balance to complete. | Remarks. |
| | No. | From. | | | | |
| 1. East of HEXHAM COPSE at foot of slope (near rusty plough).<br>Two 40-Rifle trenches, 18″ command, traversed, recessed and with head cover. Soil easy. Will probably take 7 hours. | 80 | C Co. | 40 picks<br>80 shovels | 40<br>80 | ...<br>... | |
| 2. HEXHAM COPSE. Clear.<br>Brushwood and small trees.<br>About 8,000 sq. yards.<br>Some brushwood required for trench above. | 90 | A Co. | 10 felling axes<br>70 billhooks or handaxes | 10<br>49 | ...<br>21 | *1st Dublin Fusiliers.* |
| 3. West of NORTHAM FARM at foot of slope (cleft stick and paper).<br>Two 30-Rifle trenches, 12″ command. Soil very difficult. Probably take 8 hours. | 60 | B Co. | 60 picks<br>60 shovels | 60<br>60 | ...<br>... | |
| 4. Communication trench from above trenches to east of NORTHAM FARM.<br>200 yards. Soil difficult. | 120 | D & E Cos. | 120 picks<br>120 shovels | 51<br>86 | 69<br>34 | *Use grubbers. None available. 20 only Brig. Res.* |
| &c. &c. | | | | | | |

## EARTHWORKS, &c.

1. A four hours' relief (actual digging) is long enough for the ordinary soldier. Longer reliefs, of 6 or 8 hours, may occasionally be necessary.

2. In ordinary soil, for one hour, a man can dig at the rate of 30 cub. ft. an hour; up to four hours at the rate of 20 cub. ft. per hour, or 80 cub. ft. in a four hours' relief. The normal distance at which men should be spaced apart is two paces, 5 ft.

3. The normal trace of trenches is:—Fire trench 18 ft. long, traverse 9 ft. wide, and extending about 8 ft. back with corners well rounded. The general line must be irregular, not straight, and arranged to provide flanking fire.

4. In the normal trench the fire step, 18 ins. broad, should be 4 ft. 6 ins below the crest of the parapet.

5. Behind the fire step, which should be well revetted, is a passage about 2 ft. deeper, and about 2 ft. wide at bottom. This passage, which is carried round the traverses, is therefore about 6 ft. 6 ins. below the crest.

6. How much of this cover is provided by excavation and how much by the parapet thrown up depends on the ground; if there is water near the surface, it may be necessary to build a parapet nearly 4 ft. 6 ins. high. It is then usually called a breastwork. As a rule, the parapet should be about 1 ft. to 1 ft. 6 ins. high. It must be sufficiently high to provide a good view over the ground in front.

*Earthworks, &c,*—continued.

7. A parados (back parapet) must be provided to give protection against a back burst of high explosive shell, and it should generally be a trifle higher than the front parapet, but the front slope of it should harmonise with the front slope of the parapet. Both parapet and parados tops should be uneven and not dead level.

8. If the trench is to be held for any length of time, unless the soil is very hard and well drained, trench boarding should be laid on the bottom (sole) of the trench, and the sides of trenches should be revetted. Sandbags should be used in repairs, not, if it can be avoided for new work. The back slope of the trench should not be made too steep.

9. The parapet must be bullet proof at the top; 4 ft. thickness is the minimum, 6 ft. is better.

10. An obstacle should be provided in front of the trench; this will usually be barbed wire, either stretched on posts or made up on knife-rests or in concertinas. A height of 2 ft. 6 ins. is sufficient; the near edge may be 20 yds. from the parapet. The entanglement should be 10 yds. or more broad in front of trenches that it is intended to defend for a considerable period, the entanglement should be placed in natural hollows where they exist, or if there is time and labour available broad shallow ditches should be constructed to place them in.

11. Communication trenches should give 7 ft. of cover, if possible, *e.g.*, be 5 ft. deep with 2 ft. parapet on each side. They should be traced either curved or zigzag, or with elbows or island traverses.

12. Short fire trenches should be made of some of the communication trenches to cover their flanks, and entanglements provided parallel to them; they will thus form lateral retrenchments.

13. Each company front should have at least two communication trenches between support and front line, and each battalion front if possible two between reserve and support lines, for "up" and "down" traffic.

14. Overhead cover may be classed as grenade-proof, splinter-proof and shell (5·9 in.) proof. As cover against grenades, any roofing, *e.g.*, timber or corrugated iron with 1 or 2 ft. of earth, according to its nature, is sufficient. For splinter-proof cover there might be one or more layers of pit props, 9-in. logs, rails or girders, or a foot or more of stone or bricks, or 9 ins. of concrete covered with 2 or 3 feet of earth.

15. Shell (5·9 in.) proof cover should include at least the following, counting from the top downwards:—

Thin layer of earth (6 or 9 ins.)

Bursting course of hard material (9 ins. of stones, ferro-concrete slabs, rails, or if nothing else is available, 12 ins. of broken brick, or a layer of logs).

Earth cushion, 2 to 4 ft. according to hardness.

A resting course (logs or rails wired together to form a mattress).

Earth cushion, 1½ to 3 ft. according to hardness.

Inner roof (timber, corrugated steel or iron, or concrete).

Substructure (a strong framework of brick, concrete, timber, or a corrugated steel shelter), to support the inner roof.

*Earthworks, &c.*—continued.

An air space between the inner roof and the next layer above is advisable, but the supports of the latter must not be carried on the inner roof, they should go down to the solid ground. The air in the space should have an easy means of escape to the open air.

16. In mined dugouts there should be at least 10 ft. of hard chalk or 16 ft. of Flanders' clay above the chamber, supported on strong cases or frames.

17. All deep dugouts, and others if possible, should have at least two entrances.

# 9

# SENTRIES & PATROLS

PROTECTION.

**82.** *Sentries and sentry groups.*

1. Sentries in the front line are posted in groups, which consist of from three to eight men, under a non-commissioned officer or the oldest soldier. These groups remain on duty for eight or twelve hours, and thus require no reliefs when the force is only halting for the night. In open country one man is posted as a sentry, while the remainder lie down close at hand; but if the country is close, or special precautions are necessary, the sentry post may be doubled. Sentries should always be posted double when men are very tired.

2. The distance of a sentry post from the piquet depends entirely upon the ground. Sentries should be placed so as to gain a clear view over the ground in their front, whilst concealed from the enemy's view. To avoid attracting attention, they should not be permitted to move about; on the other hand permission to lie down, except to fire, should only be given for special reasons, since sentries permitted to lie down may not remain sufficiently alert. Sentries must be made to realise the importance of their work, and their eyes and ears must always be ready to catch any indication of the presence or the movement of the enemy. Except at night, or in a fog, the bayonets of sentries should not be fixed.

3. On the approach of any person or party, a sentry will immediately warn his group. When the nearest person is within speaking distance the sentry will call out *Halt*, take cover himself, and get ready to fire. Any person not obeying the sentry, or attempting to make off after being challenged, will be fired upon without hesitation. If the order to halt is obeyed, the group commander will order the person, or one of the party, to advance and give an account of himself.

4. Sentries must know, in addition to the points mentioned in Sec. **81**:—

i. The direction of the enemy.
ii. The position of the sentries on their right and left.

iii. The position of the piquet, of neighbouring piquets, and of any detached post in the neighbourhood.
iv. The ground they have to watch.
v. How they are to deal with persons approaching their posts.
vi. Whether any friendly patrols or scouts may be expected to return through their portion of the line, and the signal, if any, by which they may be recognized.

and, by day—

vii. The names of all villages, rivers, &c., in view, and the places to which roads and railways lead.

Commanders of sentry groups must in addition know what is to be done with persons found entering or leaving the outpost line (*see* Sec. **85**). They must also be given explicit orders what to do in case of an advance in force by the enemy: whether they are to remain at their posts, which in this case must be protected from fire from behind as well as from the front, or whether they are to retire on the piquet. In the latter case they must be warned of the danger of arriving headlong on the piquet only just ahead of the enemy. In consequence of this danger such retirements are rarely permissible at night.

**83.** *Mounted piquets and vedettes.*

In addition to the principles laid down in Secs. **75** to **81** the following apply to mounted troops:—

i. Cossack posts are equivalent to sentry groups (Sec. **82**). They consist of three to six men (including the vedette), under a non-commissioned officer or sen or soldier. The vedettes, as a rule, dismount. The reliefs of the vedette always dismount, and remain as close to the vedette as possible.
ii. By night the vedette should be doubled and the post increased accordingly.
iii. Cossack posts never off-saddle, and must be ready for instant action. Piquet commanders will arrange for the necessary

feeding and watering of the horses of cossack posts. When there is no danger of surprise they may authorize the temporary removal of bits for this purpose from one-third of the horses at a time. Otherwise they should arrange for the temporary relief of a proportion of the horses.

iv. Cossack posts are relieved every 6, 12, or 24 hours, according to weather, shelter, water, &c.

v. Feeding and watering are to be carried out by one-third of a piquet or detached post at a time. Horses which are to be fed must be taken a short distance away from the others.

vi. The horses of a piquet or detached post are never to be unsaddled or unbridled at night. During the day, when matters seem quiet, girths should be loosened, and saddles shifted, one-third at a time.

### 84. *Detached posts.*

1. Detached posts from an outpost company may occasionally be necessary in front of, or to the extreme flank of, the line of resistance, to guard some spot where the enemy might collect preparatory to an attack, or which he might occupy for purposes of observation. They should only be employed in exceptional circumstances, owing to the danger of their being cut off.

2. The strength of a detached post will depend on the duty required of it, and may vary from a section to a platoon.

3. Detached posts act in the manner laid down for piquets and sentry groups. When only required for night dispositions they should not be posted till after dusk.

### 85. *Traffic through the outposts.*

1. No one other than troops on duty, prisoners, deserters, and flags of truce will be allowed to pass through the outposts either from within or from without, except with the authority of the

commander who details the outposts. Inhabitants with information will be blindfolded and detained at the nearest piquet pending instructions, and their information sent to the outpost commander.

2. No one is allowed to speak, otherwise than as directed in Sec. **82**, 3, to persons presenting themselves at the outpost line except the commander of the nearest detached post, piquet, or outpost company, who should confine his conversation to what is essential. Prisoners, and deserters, will be sent at once, under escort, through the commander of the outpost company, to the outpost commander.

**86.** *Flags of truce.*

1. On the approach of a flag of truce, one sentry, or more if at hand, will advance and halt it at such distance as to prevent any of the party who compose it overlooking the posts ; he will detain the flag of truce until instructions are received from the commander of the outpost company.

2. If permission is given for it to pass the outposts, the individuals bearing it must first be blindfolded, and then led under escort to the outpost commander. No conversation except by his permission is to be allowed on any subject, under any pretence, with the persons bearing the flag of truce.

3. If the flag of truce is merely the bearer of a letter or parcel, the commander of the outpost company must receive it, and instantly forward it to headquarters. The flag of truce, having taken a receipt, will be required forthwith to depart, and no one must be allowed to hold any conversation with the party.

**87.** *Outpost patrols.*

1. The duty of observation as defined in Sec. **75** will be carried out principally by means of patrols or standing patrols.

2. Movements of patrols through the outpost line should be as few as is consistent with the performance of this duty By day, movements through the outpost line may disclose the dispositions

of the outposts, while by night there is great danger of returning patrols being shot by their own side.

The strength of outpost patrols may be from three to eight men, under a non-commissioned officer. They may consist of mounted men, cyclists, or infantry. Patrol leaders should be given instructions before they start as to how they are to deal with inhabitants whom they may meet, and be informed, if possible, of the movements of other friendly patrols.

3. When mounted patrols are employed they should move out before it begins to get light, and patrol all approaches which an enemy might use, within distant field artillery range of the outposts.

When mounted troops are not available, infantry patrols should be sent out at this time, but it will seldom be advisable for them to reconnoitre so far from the outpost position. These patrols must remain out till after daybreak.

4. Whether mounted troops from the outpost line are patrolling to the front or not, every commander of an outpost company is responsible for his own protection against surprise. He will be informed by the outpost commander as to what mounted patrols have been sent out, and must then decide what further patrols, if any, are necessary for his own security, having due regard to the principle enunciated in para. 2 above. If mounted troops from the outpost line are patrolling to the front, it should seldom be necessary to send out infantry patrols by day, unless the country is very thick or the weather misty. At night the majority of mounted troops will be withdrawn behind the outpost line, a few standing patrols only being left out (*see* Sec. **88**), and increased vigilance will then be necessary on the part of outpost companies. It may occasionally be advisable to leave out standing infantry patrols to watch certain points in front of the outpost position, instead of sending out patrols at stated periods.

5. An outpost patrol, when going out, informs the nearest sentry of the direction it is taking, and, if possible, arranges some signal by which it may be recognized on its return. In the event of a patrol not returning when expected, another should be immediately sent

out. If a force halts for more than a day in one place, the hours at which the patrols go out (except those before sunrise), and also their route, should be changed daily.

### 88. *Standing patrols.*

Standing patrols are formed by two to eight mounted men or cyclists under a non-commissioned officer sent well in advance, to watch either the enemy, a road by which he might advance, or a locality where he could concentrate unseen. Their positions are fixed, and they remain out for several hours. They are of the utmost value, especially at night, and spare the horses, as they are not constantly in movement. The rules for cossack posts regarding off-saddling apply to standing patrols (Sec. **83**). Occasionally standing patrols are employed by infantry.

The commander of the outposts will issue orders as to the employment of standing patrols.

### 89. *Battle outposts.*

1. If the enemy is close at hand, and battle imminent, or if the battle ceases only at nightfall to be renewed next day, the whole of the troops must be in complete readiness for action. There may not even be room for outposts, and the troops will have to bivouac in their battle positions, protected only by patrols and sentries. In such cases the firing line takes the place of the piquets. It will often occur in these circumstances that no orders can be issued by superior authority as to measures of protection, and in any case nothing can relieve the commanders of advanced battalions and companies of the responsibility of securing themselves from surprise, and, unless circumstances forbid, of keeping touch with the enemy.

### 94. *Tactical reconnaissance by patrols.*

1. As the commander of a force will form his plan of action on the result of the tactical reconnaissance, officers and scouts employed on it must be highly trained, have considerable technical knowledge, be quick and intelligent observers, be possessed of judgment and determination, and, if belonging to mounted arms, be well mounted.

2. The increased range of modern firearms compels scouts to keep further away from an enemy than formerly, thus making it more difficult to see and reconnoitre; whilst the introduction of smokeless powder makes it difficult to locate him, even when his fire has been drawn. But if patrols have been in touch with the enemy during his march (when the number, strength, and distribution of his columns can be more readily ascertained), it should be possible, by comparing their reports with those of the scouts engaged in the tactical reconnaissance, to form a fairly accurate idea of the enemy's preliminary dispositions for battle.

3. General staff officers should be detailed to accompany the advanced troops in order to assist in the tactical reconnaissance, and provide the commander with such information on special points as he may require. Commanders of divisional artillery or their representatives should take part in this reconnaissance.

4. When the opposing forces are near each other, and particularly when the country is close, infantry may often be employed with advantage to attract the enemy's attention by means of surprise attacks, and so enable patrols to pass through his covering troops at other points. Cavalry should be used for these patrols when the country is suitable and mobility can be turned to good account. If the conditions are unsuited to the employment of cavalry, infantry patrols and scouts should take its place.

**95.** *The air service and aerial reconnaissance.*

(a) *Principles of employment of the air service.*

1. Field units of the Flying Corps will, as a rule, work under the direct orders of general headquarters as army troops, but aircraft may be detached to army corps or other headquarters as required, the principle being observed that the air service shall be so distributed that the units may be placed in the best positions not only to obtain information, but to co-operate with the other arms, and especially with the cavalry, in this all-important service.

2. The aircraft commander should be in close touch with the operations section of the general staff, through which he should receive his orders and to which he should act as adviser on all technical matters: *e.g.*, as to the class of aircraft to be employed on each service, and as to how far weather conditions are favourable to flight, how many aircraft should be despatched, &c.

3. Reconnoitring officers should be given the fullest information as to the military situation, and should receive clear instructions as to what information is required. They should also be given directions as to where and in what manner reports are to be made, and as to the measures that will be taken to render easily recognizable the locality where reports are to be delivered.

(b) *Method of obtaining information.*

4. The manner in which reconnaissance is to be carried out should, subject to instructions under the headings mentioned

above, be left to the discretion of those who will actually undertake the duty.

5. In clear weather, at an altitude of 5,000-6,000 feet, the presence of troops, if in the open, can be observed within a radius of four to six miles from aircraft; when nearer the earth objects will be rather more easily distinguished but will be for a shorter time in view, whilst the area under observation will be restricted. It is, therefore, best, when atmospheric conditions are favourable, to make reconnaissance from a height at which aircraft will be practically secure from fire from the ground. When the sky is wholly or partially overcast aircraft will, however, be obliged to descend near the earth for purpose of obtaining information.

(c) *Vulnerability.*

6. The most effective weapon from the ground against aircraft is the anti-aircraft gun, which throws a shell to a height of about 8,000 feet. Rifle fire is effective up to about 4,000 feet and aircraft have little to fear from it above that height. Field artillery* can be used with success against airships, but will not usually be effective against aeroplanes, owing to their rapidity and the difficulty of recognition.

7. High speed, frequent changes of direction and elevation, and movements in curves, and in a plane oblique to the horizontal, will in all circumstances reduce the probability that the enemy's guns and rifles will obtain hits. Cloud may also be used for purposes of concealment when approaching the enemy, or during reconnaissance. When resorting to such methods the pilot must always have before his mind, however, that to obtain and transmit accurate intelligence is the first consideration.

8. By far the most effective method of dealing with hostile aircraft is to attack them with armed aeroplanes.

* Howitzers, owing to the greater elevation that can be obtained, will be most dangerous. Fire from heavy guns has not been taken into consideration, as it is thought that these are unlikely to engage aircraft.

(d) *Action by troops against aircraft.*

9. In deciding whether it is advisable to open fire on aircraft, the probability of escaping observation if fire is reserved should be considered.

10. In the case of large fortresses the general position and outline of which is obvious, or when the defence of docks, or of large groups of buildings such as arsenals, workshops, storehouses, &c., is in question, the object is not concealment but to drive or keep away the enemy. Fire should, therefore, be opened as soon as the hostile aircraft are within range.

11. Troops in the field may, however, disclose their presence by opening fire against aircraft; such action therefore may facilitate reconnaissance, and fire should consequently be opened only when the prospects of obtaining results are reasonably good. Movement is easily distinguished from above. If troops lie still and are not in regular lines they are difficult to observe even in the open.

12. Aircraft form a very difficult target to fire directed from the ground, and only a small proportion of their area is vulnerable. Bullets can pass through the fabric of aeroplane wings without doing serious damage. Indiscriminate fire at hostile aircraft is, moreover, likely to cause casualties in neighbouring units, and will also disclose the position of the troops to the enemy's observer. The strictest control must be exercised over all fire directed against aircraft. In the case of rifle fire at aeroplanes, men should be instructed to aim six times the length of the machine in front, and in the case of airships at the nose of the envelope.

(e) *Intercommunication.*

13. Aircraft will be useful to supplement, in certain emergencies, other means of communication between the separated portions of an army.

When it is desired that the views of the commander-in-chief should be explained to a subordinate commander to whom direct access by road or rail is difficult or precarious, when the temporary presence is required at general headquarters of a representative of a command so situated, or when time is of importance, aircraft may also be employed for the rapid conveyance of officers between general and other headquarters.

**96.** *Reconnaissance of a position.*

1. In reconnoitring a position with a view to attack, information should be obtained on the following points:—

i. The extent of the position.
ii. The weak parts of the position.
iii. Any point or points the capture of which will facilitate the development of a searching enfilade or reverse fire against a large extent of the position, and thus render it untenable; and to what extent such point or points have been strengthened.
iv. The best line of attack, and the tactical points of which the possession will favour the development of an effective fire against the weak parts of the position.
v. Localities from which covering fire can be directed.

2. When it is intended to occupy a defensive position, the chief points to be noted are:—

i. The best distribution of the infantry, and the means of protecting the flanks.
ii. The positions for the artillery.
iii. The positions which the enemy may endeavour to seize in order to develop an effective fire against the position.
iv. The probable positions of the enemy's artillery.
v. Any points the possession of which might exert a decisive influence on the issue of the fight.
vi. The most favourable lines of attack.
vii. The most favourable ground for the counter-attack.
viii. Ground to be occupied by the general reserve, by the cavalry, and by the other mounted troops.
ix. Positions to be occupied in case of retreat.

## 97. *Reconnaissance during battle.*

When two forces are engaged the reconnaissance must be continued throughout the entire action, arrangements being always made for continuous observation of the enemy's movements and for the rapid transmission of reports. In addition to patrols working round his flanks and rear, to the work of infantry scouts, and to the cavalry action on the flanks, general staff officers, acquainted with the commander's intentions, should be posted at commanding points on the field of battle to communicate intelligence to headquarters.

## 98. *Transmission of information.*

1. The value of information depends to a great extent on the length of time that has elapsed since the events occurred to which it relates. It is of the first importance that information should be communicated with the least possible delay to the commanders for whose benefit it is intended. The authority sending out reconnoitring detachments of any kind must therefore see that the means of communication are so organized as to ensure the rapid transmission of any information which those detachments may obtain.*

An officer of the general staff with the independent cavalry should be specially charged with the duty of maintaining communication, under the direction of his commander, between the independent cavalry and army headquarters. But to save delay, arrangements should be made to transmit all really important information direct from the reconnoitring detachments to army headquarters as well as through the usual channel. It will often be found convenient to arrange for relays from the divisional cavalry for the conveyance of information from the protective cavalry (Sec. **21**).

* For the methods of transmitting information, *see* Chapter II.

# 10

# THE ATTACK

# CHAPTER VII.

## The Battle.

**99.** *Considerations which influence a commander in offering battle.*

1. **Decisive success in battle can be gained only by a vigorous offensive.** Every commander who offers battle, therefore, must be determined to assume the offensive sooner or later. If the situation be unfavourable for such a course, it is wiser, when possible, to manœuvre for a more suitable opportunity : but when superiority in skill, *moral*, or numbers has given a commander the initiative, he should turn it to account by forcing a battle before the enemy is ready. Superior numbers on the battlefield are an undoubted advantage, but skill, better organization, and training, and above all **a firmer determination in all ranks to conquer at any cost, are the chief factors of success.**

2. **Half-hearted measures never attain success in war, and lack of determination is the most fruitful source of defeat.** A commander, who has once decided either to give or to accept battle, must act with energy, perseverance, and resolution.

3. Time is an essential consideration in deciding whether an opportunity is favourable or not for decisive action. A commander who has gained a strategical advantage may have to act at once in order to prevent the enemy bringing about conditions more favourable to himself. On the other hand, ample time may be available before any change can occur in the strategical conditions, and it may then be more effective to act deliberately or to aim at manœuvring an enemy out of a strong position with a view to forcing him to fight under conditions which admit of more certain or more decisive results.

### 100. *The offensive and defensive in battle.*

1. Both opposing forces may endeavour to seize the initiative, or one may await the attack of the other. In the latter case, if victory is to be won, the defensive attitude must be assumed only in order to obtain or create a favourable opportunity for **decisive offensive action.** The original attacker may be thrown on the defensive at any time by a vigorous counter-attack; or it is open to both to fight a defensive action in one part of the field while endeavouring to force a decision by offensive action elsewhere. Thus each commander may employ defensive or offensive action to suit his requirements; the defensive being resorted to when and where it is desired to delay a decision, the offensive where it is desired to obtain one.

2. The defensive implies loss of initiative for the time being. Further, a wise choice of place and still more of the time for the eventual assumption of the offensive demands very high qualities of skill and resolution in the commander. For these reasons a defensive attitude at the outset of a battle should not be assumed except when it is advisable to gain time or to utilize advantages of ground for some special reason, *e.g.*, to compensate for inferiority of numbers. On the other hand, the commander of even a superior force may see his way to gain a decisive success with more certainty and less loss by awaiting an attack before assuming the offensive instead of attacking at once, especially if he has been able to choose and occupy deliberately a position in which he can induce the enemy to attack him. Such a position has its true value as a pivot of manœuvre. Once battle is joined the liberty of manœuvre which the initiative has conferred on the assailant is limited to what he can do with his general reserve. The defender should be able to retain equal liberty of manœuvre, if he makes skilful dispositions, resists the temptation to subordinate his movements to those of the enemy, and strikes on the first favourable opportunity. It is in the difficulty of doing this that the chief objection to allowing the enemy to take the initiative lies.

3. In the following pages the action of the two forces which meet in battle is considered under the headings, "Attack" and "Defence." It is not intended by this to imply that one force invariably attacks, and that the other invariably occupies a defensive position. Under the heading "attack" is considered the action of that force which has gained the initiative and assumes the offensive first. Under the heading "defence" is considered the action of that force which postpones the assumption of the offensive and awaits attack in the first instance. The action of a force which is content with warding off the enemy's blows, is not considered as an aspect of the battle. The methods of delaying an enemy, without seeking a decisive result, are considered under the heading "delaying action."

## THE ADVANCE TO THE BATTLEFIELD.

**101.** *Action of a force on gaining contact with the enemy.*

1. An army advances covered by its tactical advanced guards, and by the protective cavalry or by a general advanced guard, of which the protective cavalry may form part (Sec. 65, 14). At this stage collisions may be expected to occur between the opposing protective troops covering the movements of the main forces behind them. By this time, too, the independent cavalry will probably have completed any special strategical missions assigned to it, and, if so, should usually be available to assist in defeating the hostile advanced troops, and in reconnoitring and hampering the enemy's main columns. Success in these preliminary combats will retain for a commander the initiative he has gained, or regain it for him if it has been lost; it will gain him strategic liberty of action, and will thereby enable him to act with certainty and impose his will upon the enemy. **The defeat of the hostile advanced troops is, however, only a means towards the subsequent destruction of the enemy's main force on the battlefield, and this ultimate object must be held in view.**

2. So soon as the cavalry, assisted, if necessary, by the other arms (Sec. **92**), has driven in the enemy's advanced troops, the information thus obtained, combined with information received from other sources, should enable the commander of the force to review the strategical situation, and to decide definitely whether to manœuvre to gain time, avoiding an engagement; whether to attack the enemy; or whether to await attack.

3. When contact with the enemy is anticipated, it is advisable that commanders of columns should be well forward, usually with their advanced guards. They will then be in a position to obtain earlier and more accurate information regarding the enemy and the tactical features of the ground, to make the most rapid and suitable dispositions to meet tactical situations as they occur, to influence effectively the action of the advanced guard in accordance with the intentions of the commander of the force, and, in the case of a general engagement, to carry out the deployment with the least delay.

### **102.** *Deployment for action.*

1. When the commander has decided to accept battle, the various columns composing the force will be directed, whilst still in their march formations, towards the area in which they are to act. As a rule the columns should not leave their march formations until the commander has formed his plan of battle, or until the action of the advanced troops shows that deployment is necessary (*see* Sec. **23**).

2. Before deploying it will usually be desirable for each column to close up and assume a formation of assembly. When time presses it may be necessary to move units directly from the line of march into their position in the deployed line, but this is likely to result in troops being employed piecemeal, and the occasion must be very urgent to justify a commander in abandoning the advantages which systematic arrangements for a concerted advance confer. It is important that the deployment should be concealed

from the enemy by the action of the advanced troops. It will often be advisable to reinforce the latter with sufficient artillery to cover the deployment of the troops in rear.

3. The principles upon which the troops are disposed will depend upon the commander's plans. **The first object of a commander who seeks to gain the initiative in battle is to develop superiority of fire as a preparation for the delivery of a decisive blow.** The commander must decide whether the direction of the decisive blow is to be pre-determined or to be left open until the situation has been developed by preparatory action. Broadly speaking, success in battle may be sought by means of a converging movement of separated forces so timed as to strike the enemy's front and flank, or flanks, simultaneously, few, if any, reserves being retained in hand by the commander-in-chief; or a part of the force only may be employed in a preparatory action while the commander keeps the remainder, known as the general reserve, in his own hands with which eventually to force the decision.

A decisive attack against some portion of the enemy's front offers a possibility of breaking his army in two and may give great and far-reaching results. The long range, accuracy, and rapidity of fire of modern weapons reduce, however, the chances of success of such an attack, while failure may result in the attacking force being enveloped and destroyed. It will usually, therefore, be wiser to direct the decisive effort against one of the enemy's flanks, the choice of objective being made either before or after deployment according to circumstances. The development of fire effect is usually facilitated when the plan of battle has for its object the envelopment of one or, if in very superior strength, of both the enemy's flanks.

The character of the opposing commander, the relative numbers, fighting value, and manœuvring power of the opposing forces, as well as the ground and the strategical situation, are all factors which must be weighed in determining the general form in which the battle is to be fought.

As a general principle the greater the fighting power and the offensive spirit of his adversary, the more advisable will it be for a commander to engage him effectively along his whole front, while adequately covering his own communications, before attempting to force a final decision. Furthermore, any separation of forces in face of a skilful and resolute opponent will be dangerous unless in such strength that each of the separated portions can neither be overwhelmed by the enemy nor so delayed by a detachment as to give him an opportunity of attacking them in detail. On the other hand a commander may by skilfully disposing or manœuvring a general reserve be able to strike successfully at his opponent's flank without separating his own forces during the advance to the battlefield and the deployment for action. With very small forces when both the battlefield and the general reserve are proportionately small it may be possible to place the latter in a central position from which it can be brought into action at the right time and place. With large forces there can be little, if any, hope of being able to strike with the general reserve at the right moment unless the approximate area in which it is to be used is determined in time. In such circumstances, therefore, it will generally be necessary to decide, either at the time when the plans for the deployment are being formed, or, at any rate, soon after deployment where the decision will be forced, and to place the general reserve accordingly.

## THE ATTACK.

### 103. *General principles.*

1. It is seldom either possible or desirable to attempt to overwhelm an enemy everywhere. The object will usually be to concentrate as large a force as possible against one decisive point, to deliver the decisive attack, while the remainder is employed to prepare the way for this attack, by attracting the enemy's attention, holding him to the ground, and wearing down his power of resistance. The term decisive attack does not imply that the

influence of other attacks is indecisive, but rather that it is the culmination of gradually increasing pressure relentlessly applied to the enemy at all points from the moment when contact with him is first obtained.

2. **The objective of the decisive attack should be struck unexpectedly and in the greatest possible strength.**

**104.** *Preliminary measures.*

1. It will frequently happen that a suitable moment for the decisive attack will be found only after long and severe fighting. For this reason systematic arrangements for obtaining, sifting, and transmitting information throughout the battle are important. The information upon which the commander of the force will base his original deployment will usually be obtained by preliminary reconnaissance (Sec. **92**), though it may be possible to obtain sufficient data as to an enemy's strength and intentions to enable the commander to decide approximately where eventually to launch his decisive attack before any tactical reconnaissance has been completed.

2. The commander of the force and subordinate commanders will be guided by the following principles in framing orders for an attack :—

i. A definite objective or task should be assigned to each body of troops, the actual limits of frontage being specified as far as possible. Each body of troops thus assigned to a distinct tactical operation should be placed under one commander.

ii. The direction of the attack to be made by each body of troops should be distinctly stated.

iii. Most careful arrangements should be made to ensure that attacks intended to be simultaneous should be so in reality.

iv. The choice of the manner in which the task assigned to each body of troops is to be performed should be left to its commander.

Each commander who issues orders should assemble his subordinate commanders, if possible, in view of the ground over which the troops are to operate, explain his orders, and satisfy himself that they thoroughly understand their respective tasks.

3. The conditions which affect the question of the frontage to be allotted to the various parts of an attacking force must vary with the circumstances of each battle. Ground, time conditions, the information available, the relative value of the opposing troops, the possibility of gaining a surprise, are some of the inconstant factors to be weighed. It is, therefore, neither possible nor desirable to give more than general indications as to how the problem is to be solved. **The general principle is that the enemy must be engaged in sufficient strength to pin him to his ground, and to wear down his power of resistance, while the force allotted to the decisive attack must be as strong as possible.** The higher the fighting qualities of the enemy are estimated, the more closely must he be engaged. It may be taken that against an enemy of approximately equal fighting value, where the attacking artillery is slightly superior, a force fully equal to that of the enemy holding the position* (excluding his probable general reserve) is the least that will suffice for this purpose. Such a force, which should ordinarily be divided into firing line and supports, with local reserves, would be disposed in varying strength along the front, according to the nature of the ground, the frontage varying from one man to three or more men per yard. The decisive blow must be driven home. The latest experience goes to show that a smaller force than from three to five men per yard on the front on which the decisive attack is to be delivered will rarely prove sufficient, this force being distributed in such depth as circumstances make advisable.

4. As the opposing forces draw near, the cavalry will be unable to remain in the front line ; it will therefore be allotted one or more positions of readiness, where it can best act in accordance with the

* This force may be roughly estimated from the data given in Sec. **108.**

commander-in-chief's plan, and from which it can easily deploy either to exploit a success gained by the other arms or to support them in case of a check. Artillery should be so distributed as to be able to support the infantry when required. Where artillery forms part of a unit allotted to the general reserve it will usually be given a special rôle by the commander-in-chief, except when the general reserve is required to carry out or complete a wide enveloping movement, when it will be accompanied by its complement of artillery.

5. During an engagement the position of a commander will depend a great deal on the size of the force he commands (*see* Sec. **93**). With a small force it may be possible to exercise personal supervision, but with very large forces the commander-in-chief should usually be well in rear, beyond the reach of distraction by local events, and in signal communication with his chief subordinates (Sec. **17**). Subordinate commanders should take up positions where they can obtain a good view of the area in which their commands are operating, and which admit of easy communication with their immediate superior and the units under their command. Should a commander leave the position to which he has directed that reports are to be sent, a staff officer must be detailed to receive and forward all reports and orders that may come in.

### **105.** *The general conduct of the attack.*

1. Under the protection of the advanced guard, the artillery will take such preparatory steps as will enable it to support the advanced guard and open fire on such targets as the tactical situation demands. As a general principle, fire should not be opened with more guns than are necessary to accomplish the task in hand, the remainder being kept in positions of readiness.

2. Artillery on the battlefield is generally protected by the distribution of the other arms. When, however, guns are in an exposed position, an escort should be detailed, and if this has not been done, it is the duty of the artillery commander concerned to

apply to the commander of the nearest troops, who must provide an escort. This escort, whose duty it is to protect the guns from surprise, should consist, when possible, of mounted men in the case of field artillery, and of infantry in the case of heavy and mountain artillery.

A superior officer who orders guns into action is responsible that they are provided with a suitable escort if the situation demands it. The senior officer present, whether artillery commander or escort commander, will issue the necessary instructions to the escort, but the commander of the escort must in either case have a free hand in carrying them out.

3. The object of artillery fire is to help the infantry to maintain its mobility and offensive power. Artillery commanders must therefore keep touch with the infantry commanders whose attack they are supporting, in order that the fire of their batteries may be directed against what, for the time being, are the most important targets from the infantry point of view. When a division is employed upon more than one tactical operation and the efforts of the whole cannot be directly combined, it will be advisable to form artillery and infantry temporarily into groups, under commanders each charged with the conduct of one distinct operation.

4. The advance of the firing line must be characterized by **the determination to press forward at all costs.** In order to prevent the enemy from thinning his line so as to reinforce the point against which he expects the decisive attack will be directed, and to force him to use up his reserves, it will be absolutely necessary for the troops, to whom the rôle of wearing down the enemy's resistance is allotted, to act with vigour. No half-measures will succeed. The enemy must be deceived, and this will call for as much self-sacrifice and devotion on the part of these troops as will be required from those taking part in the decisive attack. When once the firing line comes under effective fire, its further advance will be chiefly assisted by the covering fire of artillery, machine guns, and special detachments of infantry detailed for this duty. The various portions of the firing line will also on occasions

be able to afford each other mutual support by fire, and all commanders must be on the alert to assist units on their flanks in this manner when the situation requires. Mutual support in the firing line will, as a rule, however, be more automatic than deliberately arranged, and in no case must its employment be allowed to induce hesitation in the advance. The paramount duty of all leaders in the firing line is to get their troops forward, and if every leader is imbued with a determination to close with the enemy he will be unconsciously assisting his neighbour also, for as a rule the best method of supporting a neighbouring unit is to advance. The artillery fire must be distributed according to requirements on all objectives from which effective fire is being brought to bear on the attacking infantry. Quick-firing guns cannot maintain a rapid fire throughout a battle. Artillery should, therefore, use rapid fire when the infantry firing line is seen to be in need of assistance to enable it to advance; infantry should take advantage of periods of rapid artillery fire to gain ground. Aided in this way the infantry will fight its way forward to close range, and, in conjunction with the artillery and machine guns, will endeavour to gain superiority of fire. This will involve a gradual building up of the firing line in good fire positions, usually within close infantry range of the enemy. Here it is to be expected that there will be a prolonged and severe fire fight, during which each side will try to exhaust its opponent's power of endurance and force him to use up his reserves, while keeping its own intact.

5. The attack on each tactical point will constitute a distinct engagement in itself, and may require a large number of men and guns. Thus the attack, more often than not, will resolve itself into a series of distinct engagements, each raging round a different locality, and each possibly protracted over many hours. All important tactical points, such as suitable buildings, small woods, &c., should, when required, at once be put in a state of defence, so that attempts on the part of the enemy to recapture them may be defeated, and that they may serve as supporting

points to the attack. Local reserves will often find opportunities for strengthening localities or fire positions which have been gained by the firing line, and to assist them in this, detachments of engineer field companies may be attached to them with advantage. Machine guns will be specially valuable in bringing a sudden fire to bear from such positions, both in order to cover a further advance and to assist in defeating counter-attacks. Machine guns can normally support an attack most efficiently from well concealed positions provided with good cover, and within effective infantry range of the enemy. Occasionally, when good opportunities for a concealed advance present themselves, they may be established within close infantry range of the objective.

6. Infantry in attack must not delay the advance or diminish the volume of fire by entrenching. Entrenchments in the attack are only used when, owing to further advance being impossible, the efforts of the attacking force must temporarily be limited to holding the ground already won. The advance must be resumed at the first possible moment.

### **106.** *The decisive attack.*

1. The development of the battle should enable the commander to make up his mind when and where to deliver the decisive attack, if he has not done so before (*see* Sec. **102**). The general reserve, if not already in position, will accordingly be moved there, **as secretly as possible.** The launching of the general reserve in the attack will be the signal for the application of the greatest possible pressure against the enemy's whole front; every man, horse, and gun, whether belonging to the general reserve or not, must co-operate in completing the enemy's overthrow.

2. As the crisis of the battle approaches, and the enemy becomes morally and physically exhausted, the chances of successful cavalry action increase. For effective intervention the concentration of as large a part of the cavalry as possible is required; the rest depends chiefly upon the cavalry commander, who should be where he can best watch the progress of events, keep in touch

## THE ACTION OF SHRAPNE

TIME FUSE SHRAPNEL.—The shell, fired from gun at
latter and about 15 feet above the ground. T

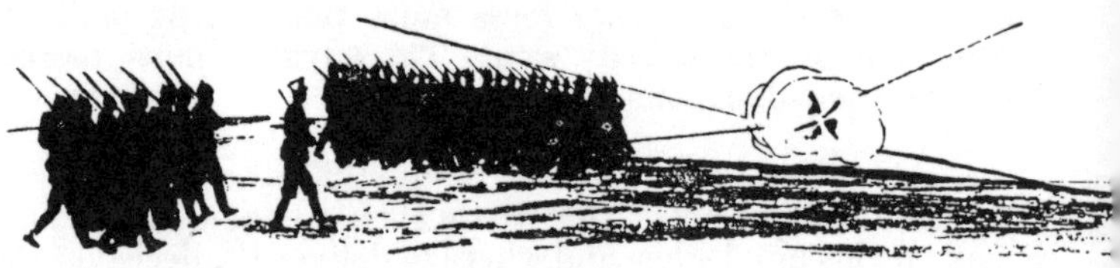

PERCUSSION SHRAPNEL.—The shell, fired from gun
throwing a shower of bullets at approaching men. It

CASE (SHRAPNEL) SHOT.—Used at short range again
200 yards range t

# :XPLAINED IN DIAGRAM.

ːnst entrenched infantry, bursts about 80 yards in front of the
.ines indicate the zone covered by the bullets.

ıgainst advancing infantry, bursts upon hitting the ground,
.ed against buildings, but is ineffective on soft ground.

The shell bursts immediately after leaving the gun. At
pread is 25 yards.

with other commanders, and carry out the instructions of the commander-in-chief, with whom he should be in signal communication (if possible by telephone) When a favourable opportunity for cavalry action arises, it must be seized at once; but it is important that the result should promise to **have a direct influence upon the decision of the battle**, and that cavalry should not be exposed to heavy losses and horses be exhausted on minor enterprises. The attacking infantry should take immediate advantage of the results of the cavalry action.

3. In selecting the objective of the decisive attack, a commander must consider whether he can develop the full power of his artillery against it. An objective which may appear at first sight easy of access to the infantry, may prove in the end costly to attack, if it does not lend itself to the judicious application of artillery fire; and *vice versâ*, localities which present difficulties to the infantry alone may, if it is possible to bring the converging fire of artillery to bear on them, be carried with comparatively little loss.

4. The principle of the employment of artillery in the battle is that **the greater the difficulties of the infantry, the more fully should the fire power of the artillery be developed.** As the infantry advances to the decisive attack, every effort should be made to bring a converging artillery fire to bear on its immediate objective, and artillery fire will be continued until it is impossible for the artillery to distinguish between its own and the enemy's infantry. The danger from shells bursting short is more than compensated for by the support afforded, if fire is maintained to the last moment; but in order to reduce this danger, it is the duty of artillery commanders to keep themselves informed as to the progress of their infantry, and to discontinue fire against the objective of the assault when the infantry is getting to close quarters if such fire cannot be readily observed and controlled. A portion of the artillery must be pushed forward so as to be able to deal with possible counter-attacks, and to give the infantry immediate assistance, when the fluctuations of the fight make this necessary.

5. **The climax of the infantry attack is the assault, which is made possible by superiority of fire.** The fact that superiority of fire has been obtained will usually be first observed from the firing line; it will be known by the weakening of the enemy's fire, and perhaps by the movements of individuals or groups of men from the enemy's position towards the rear. The impulse for the assault must therefore often come from the firing line, and it is the duty of any commander in the firing line who sees that the moment for the assault has arrived, to carry it out, and for all other commanders to co-operate.

Should it be necessary to give the impulse for the assault from the rear, all available reinforcements will be thrown into the fight, and as they reach the firing line, will carry it with them and rush the position.

6. It will often happen that opportunities for closing with the enemy will arise at other points of the battlefield than where the decisive attack is being delivered. When such an assault is successful, troops on the flanks must endeavour at once to widen the breach made in the enemy's position and to confirm the advantage gained. Such an opening should be seized at once, and a local assault delivered. The result of effecting a lodgment in a portion of the position will be to weaken the defender's hold on the remainder, and may even force him to fall back along his whole line. Troops who have thus penetrated the line of defence must at once prepare to meet a local counter-attack, for the enemy will probably endeavour to recover the ground which has been lost.

7. If, during the attack, the enemy attempts to counter-attack, the troops threatened should hold on and endeavour to gain time. As a rule the most effective counter-measure will be to press the decisive attack with renewed vigour, for **success at the vital point will mean ultimate success at all points.**

8. It may be found impossible during one day to establish a sufficient superiority of fire to justify an assault being delivered. Should this be the case, the night should be employed in bringing artillery forward and providing cover for the guns, whilst the

firing line should be re-organized, or relieved by fresh troops if possible, its cover improved, and, if necessary, a further advance made with a view to a resumption of the fight under more favourable conditions at dawn (Sec. **134**). In continuous operations of this nature, the powers of endurance of the troops must be considered.

9. After a successful assault immediate steps must be taken to get the attacking infantry in hand for the work that lies before them. A portion of the troops must at once be pushed forward to harry the retreating forces, while the remainder are being re-formed, under their own officers, if possible, in preparation for a relentless pursuit. Owing to the possibility of hostile gun-fire being brought to bear on the captured position, units should not be re-formed on the position itself, but should move forward to the least exposed localities available. Steps must also be taken to meet a possible counter-attack. Some artillery should be sent rapidly forward to the captured position to assist in this work, to break down any resistance that may be offered from a second position, and to support the pursuit. Field companies of engineers should also be moved forward to strengthen the position against counter-attack or improve the communications in case of necessity. Meanwhile the cavalry should exploit to the full the opportunities created for it by the successful action of the other arms.

40/W.O./4188.

**11. A.**

# QUESTIONS A PLATOON COMMANDER SHOULD ASK HIMSELF BEFORE AN ATTACK.

1. Do I know exactly what objectives have been allotted (a) to my platoon, (b) to my Company, (c) to my Battalion? Have I a map showing them?

2. Have I explained them to my N.C.Os. and men? And have I given my N.C.Os. a sketch-plan of the platoon's objective?

3. Do my N.C.Os. and men understand exactly what formation the platoon is adopting for this attack, and the various duties each one of them has to perform? How am I using my Lewis gun?

4. Do I know the bearings both of the left and of the right of my objective?

5. Do I know, and do my N.C.Os. and men know, the names of the units on my flanks?

6. Do I understand the barrage lines and timing of lifts in the Artillery Programme?

7. Have I impressed upon my men the great importance of keeping close up to our own barrage?

8. Is my watch synchronised?

9. Do I understand all orders sufficiently to be able to take command of the Company if my Company Commander gets knocked out?

(11653.) Wt. W 3760—9842. 20,000. 6/17. D & S. G 2. P17/433.

## 2

10. Have I told my Platoon Sergeant and N.C.Os. everything I can to enable them to carry on if I get knocked out?

11. Are all my N.C.Os. and men properly equipped according to orders?

12. Do I know who have (a) wire-cutters, (b) Very pistols and lights?

13. Have (a) bombs, (b) flares been issued to each man, and orders about their carriage and use properly explained?

14. Do I know and does my Orderly know, (a) the best way to Company Headquarters now; (b) how to find my Company Commander during and after the attack; (c) where Battalion Headquarters is, and, if it is moving, at what stage and to what place?

15. Have I warned my men to shoot or bayonet anyone giving the order "Retire"?

16. Have I told them that slightly-wounded men must carry back their equipment, and that men must on no account weaken the line by taking back wounded?

17. Do the stretcher-bearers know their way to the advanced dressing station and the arrangements made for getting away wounded?

18. Do I know what to do with prisoners?

19. Have I detailed the patrol to be pushed out as soon as the objective has been gained, and explained to it exactly what to do?

20. Do my men understand the necessity of establishing touch with units on my flanks, or, if on gaining our objective we are not in touch, of establishing blocks immediately?

3

21. Do I understand that to consolidate a well-defined target exposes my men to heavy shelling afterwards? Have I thought out where and how it is best to consolidate the objective I am about to attack?

22. Do all my men know which are UP and which are DOWN communication trenches?

23. Do I know and have I explained to my N.C.Os. the arrangements for supply of water, S.A.A., bombs, sandbags, wire, &c.

24. Have I made all possible arrangements for any special work required from my platoon after the objective has been gained?

25. What is the S.O.S. signal?

---

**B.**

## QUESTIONS A PLATOON COMMANDER SHOULD ASK HIMSELF WHEN THE OBJECTIVE HAS BEEN GAINED.

1. Am I and my men where they were meant to be?
2. Have I reported my position and the situation generally?
3. Are flares being lit when called for by the contact aeroplane?

4

4. Is my platoon reorganised to resist counter-attack ?

5. Am I doing all I can to consolidate the position and am I consolidating in the best place ?

6. Am I in touch with units on my flanks ? If not, are blocks being established as quickly as possible ?

7. Is the Lewis gun disposed to the best advantage ? Does it cover a block ?

8. Has the patrol been pushed out as I arranged ?

9. Am I making the best use of my scouts and snipers ?

10. What is the enemy doing ? Am I doing all in my power to find out, and to let my Company Commander have the information as quickly as possible ?

11. What special orders did I receive ? Was I ordered to dig any part of a communication trench ? If so, are the men told off for the work working at it ?

12. Can I put up anything as a guide to our position for the artillery ?

13. Do I appreciate that if my present position is unhealthy it is likely to be much worse if I try to withdraw ?

Do I understand that bold and energetic action makes for success ?

# 11

# GAS!

# STANDING ORDERS FOR DEFENCE AGAINST GAS.

## 1.—GAS ZONES.

Armies will define the limits of three zones in their respective areas known respectively as the Alert, Ready and Precautionary Zones.

The approximate extent of these Zones will be as follows:—

| | |
|---|---|
| Alert Zone ... | Within about two miles of of the front line, and within those areas behind that limit especially exposed to gas shelling. |
| Ready Zone ... | Beyond about two miles but within five miles of the front line. |
| Precautionary Zone | Beyond about five miles but within twelve miles of the front line. |

The limits of these zones will be indicated by notice boards on all main roads.

## 2.—CARRIAGE OF RESPIRATORS.

(i.) *Within the Alert Zone* the Box Respirator will always be carried in the "Alert" position. It will be worn outside all clothing, and nothing will be slung across the chest in such a way as to interfere with the quick adjustment of the Respirator. The chin strap of the steel helmet will be worn on the *point* of the chin.

(ii.) *Within the Ready Zone* a Box Respirator will always be carried.

(iii.) *Within the Precautionary Zone* a Box Respirator *or* a P.H. Helmet will always be carried.

(iv.) The P.H. Helmet will not be carried in the Alert or Ready Zones.

(v.) Military Police will be instructed to report all cases of infringement of the above orders.

**3.—GENERAL PRECAUTIONARY MEASURES.**

A. *Within the Alert Zone* the following rules will be observed :—

(i.) Box Respirators will be inspected *daily.*

(ii.) Gas N.C.O.s will inspect daily all gas alarm appliances and anti-gas stores. They will see that gas proof dug-outs are in good order, and that blankets are kept moist.

(iii.) Sentries will always be posted over Strombos Horns to give warning of a cloud gas attack. All other sentries will act as Gas Sentries, and will be provided with an alarm appliance to give warning in case of gas shelling or of a cloud attack.

(iv.) Each Sentry group will have a definite area to alarm in the event of a gas attack or bombardment.

(v.) Sentries must be posted to give warning to men in dug-outs.

(vi.) All working parties of 10 or more men, not working in the immediate vicinity of a sentry, will have a special sentry posted to give warning in the event of gas being used by the enemy.

(vii.) Precautions will be taken to protect ammunition from the corrosive action of gas, *vide* instructions given in S.S. 534.

(viii.) Stores of fuel will be kept for clearing dug-outs.

(ix.) Units in the line will make wind observations, and sentries will be warned to be on the alert for signs of cloud gas whenever the wind is in a dangerous quarter.

(x.) All cellars, dug-outs, etc., occupied by sleeping troops will be made gas-proof; and men will always wear the respirator in the alert position when sleeping.

B. *In the Ready and Precautionary Zones* the following rules will be observed:—

(i.) Anti-gas appliances will be inspected at least once a week and immediately before men proceed to any point within the Alert Zone.

(ii.) All sentries, traffic control men, military police, etc., when on duty, will act as gas sentries, and will be provided with suitable alarm devices where necessary.

(iii.) Men may be allowed to take off their respirators when sleeping, but must keep them within reach.

(iv.) Arrangements will be made by Commanders of units and Area Commandants to communicate a gas alarm rapidly to all ranks.

## 4.—ACTION TO BE TAKEN IN THE EVENT OF AN ENEMY GAS SHELL OR T.M. BOMBARDMENT.

(i.) At the first sign of gas shell of any kind or on hearing the alarm, the breath must be held and the respirator adjusted immediately without waiting until the presence of gas is recognised.

(ii.) The alarm will be spread immediately to all troops in the neighbourhood:—

(*a*) By gongs and rattles.

(*b*) By shouting "Gas shells"—after the respirator has been adjusted.

(*c*) By runners where necessary.

Strombos Horns will *not* be used.

Men in dug-outs, observation posts and mine shafts must be warned, and sleeping men roused.

(iii.) Gas proof dug-outs will be closed immediately, and any fires burning in such dug-outs put out. Care must be taken that men do not enter protected dug-outs if their clothing is contaminated with gas.

(iv.) Sentries will be posted at suitable points to warn men to put on their respirators before entering the shelled area. These sentries will not be withdrawn until the area is free from gas.

**Action after a Gas Shell or T.M. Bombardment.**

(v.) *Respirators will be worn until permission to remove them is given by an officer.*

(vi.) Gas may remain in liquid form on the ground for several hours after a bombardment. When it is impossible to withdraw men from an infected area, respirators will be worn until the ground is clear. Gas shell holes will be covered with fresh earth when possible.

(vii.) Closed spaces such as dug-outs and cellars may retain gas for several hours, and must be cleared by means of fires. Men will not enter such places without wearing respirators until permission has been given by an officer.

(viii.) When a man is close to the burst of a gas shell his clothes may become contaminated with liquid. When possible the clothes will be removed and exposed to the air. Care must be taken that men sleeping in closed spaces are not gassed by long exposure to small quantities of gas brought in on their clothing or equipment.

(ix.) Men affected by gas will be spared all exertion, and, if possible, will be carried to the nearest Aid Post or Dressing Station.

(x.) Transport will move from the shelled area when possible.

## 5.—ACTION TO BE TAKEN IN THE EVENT OF AN ENEMY CLOUD GAS ATTACK.

**The Alarm.**

(i.) Alarm will at once be given by all means available :—By Strombos Horns, gongs, rattles, telephone, and, if necessary, by orderly.

Sentries will warn all ranks in the trenches, dug-outs, observation posts or mine-shafts.

(ii.) Sentries on Strombos Horns will sound the horn. (*a*) When they detect *cloud* gas; (*b*) when they hear other Strombos Horns sounding. Strombos Horns will *not* take up the alarm from gongs and rattles.

(iii.) In order to restrict the spread of false alarms, when possible Strombos Horns in the *Precautionary* zone will be placed so that they need not be sounded until the alarm is confirmed by telephone.

(iv.) Should the gas cloud be unaccompanied by an Infantry attack, no S.O.S. signal will be sent, but the letters G.A.S. will be telephoned or telegraphed, followed by the name of the trench opposite to which the gas is being liberated.

This message will not be sent in case of a gas shell bombardment only.

(v.) Arrangements will be made for an immediate report of a hostile gas attack to be sent to all formations within 20 miles, giving the map reference of the point of attack, as follows:—

Divisions will warn—

Corps H.Q.

All other Divisions of the same Corps. (If a flank Division) neighbouring Divisions of adjoining Corps.

Corps will warn—

Army H.Q.

All other Corps of same Army. (If a flank Corps) neighbouring Corps of adjoining Army.

(vi.) Arrangements will be made for the warning to be repeated where necessary, to an officer in each village or camp within a radius of 20 miles of the point of attack, who will be responsible for warning units billeted there.

(vii.) Armies and Corps will arrange to warn civil authorities within their respective areas, who are responsible for the protection and warning of all civilians.

**Action on the Alarm being given.**

(viii.) *There should be as little movement and talking as possible.* All ranks will at once adjust their Small Box Respirators. Men in dug-outs will do so before leaving dug-outs.

(ix.) The blanket curtains of protected dug-outs and cellars will be properly adjusted, and fires in such dug-outs put out.

(x.) Troops in the front lines, and wherever the tactical situation demands, will stand to arms.

(xi.) In rear lines there is no objection, where the tactical situation permits, to troops, with the exception of sentries and of officers and N.C.O.s on duty, remaining in dug-outs.

(xii.) All bodies of troops or transport on the move will halt, and working parties will cease work until the gas cloud has passed.

(xiii.) If a relief is in progress, units should stand steady as far as possible until the gas cloud has passed.

(xiv.) Supports and parties bringing up ammunition and grenades will only be moved up if the tactical situation demands.

**Action during an enemy cloud gas attack.**

(xv.) The troops in the front trenches will open a slow rate of rifle fire at once against the enemy's trenches, and occasional short bursts will be fired from machine guns to ensure that all weapons are in working order.

(xvi.) Corps will arrange a suitable artillery programme to be carried out in the event of a cloud gas attack.

**Action after an enemy cloud gas attack.**

(xvii.) Trenches will be cleared of gas with anti-gas fans and sandbags.

(xviii.) Respirators will be worn until permission to remove them is given by an officer.

(xix.) *A sharp look-out will be maintained for a repetition of the attack as long as the wind continues in a dangerous quarter. Men will sleep on the fire-step within reach of a sentry.*

(xx.) The instructions given in Section 5 (iii.) above, with regard to entering dug-outs, etc., will be observed.

(xxi.) Men affected by gas will be spared all exertion and, if possible, will be carried to the nearest Aid Post or Dressing Station.

(xxii.) After a gas attack, troops in the front trenches are to be relieved of all fatigue and carrying work for 24 hours, by sending up working parties from companies in the rear.

(xxiii.) Horses which have been exposed to the gas will not be worked for 24 hours if it can be avoided.

(xxiv.) Rifles and machine guns must be cleaned after a gas attack. Oil cleaning will prevent corrosion for 12 hours, but the first opportunity must be taken to clean all parts in boiling water containing a little soda.

(xxv.) S.A.A. must be carefully examined. All rounds affected by the gas must be replaced by new cartridges immediately, and will be cleaned.

(xxvi.) Expended air cylinders of Strombos Horns will be replaced by full ones.

### 6.—ANTI-GAS TRENCH STORES.

(i.) These comprise :—

Strombos Horns and other alarm devices.
Wind Vanes.
Gas-proof coverings for dug-outs.
Anti-gas fans.
Stores of fuel for clearing dug-outs.
Vermorel Sprayers.
Gas sampling apparatus.

(ii.) Commanders of formations or units relieving one another are responsible that these are duly handed over and taken over.

(iii.) The actual taking over should be done by Company (Battery) Gas N.C.O.s, who will go up with the advanced party (if possible in daylight) for this purpose. They will report any defects to their Company (Battery) Commander.

(iv.) Divisional Gas Officers will make arrangements for the weekly inspection of all anti-gas trench stores. Commanding Officers should take this opportunity of bringing to the notice of the Divisional Gas Officer or his N.C.O.s any trench stores which are deficient or damaged.

# 12

# MISCELLANEOUS

# ORGANIZATION AND DEFINITIONS.

## i. *Organization.*

1. An infantry brigade consists of :—
   Headquarters.
   4 Infantry battalions.

2. A battalion consists of :—
   Headquarters.
   Machine gun section.
   4 companies.

For purposes of administration the details of battalion headquarters (other than the battalion commander, senior major, adjutant, and quartermaster) and the machine gun section are posted to companies as supernumerary to the establishment of platoons. Their distribution among the companies is at the discretion of the battalion commander but should be so arranged that the number of supernumeraries in each company is approximately equal.

3. A company consists of 4 platoons*, and is commanded by a major or mounted captain, with a captain as second in command.

4. A platoon consists of 4 sections, and is commanded by a subaltern, with a serjeant as second in command (platoon serjeant). Platoons are numbered consecutively throughout the battalion from 1 to 16.

---

* In certain battalions with a special establishment the number of platoons in a company varies from two to four.

When a subaltern is not available to command, the platoon serjeant will take his place, but in this case a section commander will not be taken from his command to act as platoon serjeant. The transfer of a platoon serjeant to another platoon should be as infrequent as possible.

So far as the exigencies of peace conditions will admit, this organization will be maintained both in barracks and in the field for all duties, including the detailing of fatigues. The men will thus acquire the spirit of comradeship, and learn to repose confidence in each other, while the section commanders will be accustomed to command, and to act when necessary on their own judgment.

5. A section is commanded by a non-commissioned officer, and is the normal fire-unit. Sections are numbered consecutively throughout the company from 1 to 16, and the men of each section should be kept together in barracks as well as in the field. The post of section commander is a definite appointment, and transfers should be as infrequent as possible.

## ii. *Definitions.*

*Alignment.*—Any straight line on which a body of troops is formed, or is to form.

*Column.*—Bodies of troops on parallel and successive alignments, at a distance from one another equal to their own frontage, *e.g.* column of companies or column of platoons.

*Column of masses.*—See under masses.

*Column of route.*—A column of fours with not more than four men abreast in any part of the column, including officers and supernumeraries. The normal formation for troops marching on a road.

*Close column.*—A column with distances reduced to suit requirements. If no specific orders are given, the distance between units will be seven paces.

*Double column.*—Two parallel columns, with any named interval between them.

*Deploy, to.*—To change formation from column or close column into line on the same alignment.

*Depth.*—The space occupied by a body of troops from front to rear.

*Direction (battalion, company, platoon, section, or file of).*—The battalion, company, platoon, section, or file responsible for keeping the direction in a drill movement.

*Distance.*—The space between units in column or close column, measured from the heels of the front rank of one unit to the heels of the front rank of the next.

*Dress, to.*—To take up the alignment correctly.

*Drill.*—The training of the soldier to execute certain movements as a second nature.

*Echelon.*—A formation of successive and parallel units facing in the same direction, each on a flank and to the rear of the unit in front of it.

*File.*—A front rank man and his rear rank man.

*Fire unit.*—Any number of men firing by the executive command of one. The section is the normal fire unit.

*Flank, directing.*—The flank by which units march or dress.

*Flank, inner.*—That nearer to the directing flank.

*Flank, outer.*—That opposite to the inner or directing flank.

*Formation (Battalion, company, platoon, section, or file of).*—The battalion, company, platoon, section, or file on which a change of formation is based.

*Frontage.*—The extent of ground covered laterally by troops.

*In action (of a machine gun).*—A machine gun is said to be in action when it is mounted, loaded, and laid, not necessarily firing.

*Incline.*—The movement by which ground is gained to the front and flank simultaneously.

*Interval.*—The lateral space between units on the same alignment.

*Interval, deploying.*—The lateral space between units in close column or in column, on the same alignment, the space being equal to the frontage of a unit in line.

*Line.*—Troops formed on the same alignment.

*Mass.*—A battalion with its companies in line of close columns of platoons, with five paces interval between companies and seven paces distance be ween platoons.

*Mass, open.*—A battalion with its companies in line of columns of platoons, with five paces interval between companies.

*Masses, column of.*—Battalions in mass, on parallel and successive alignments, with any named distance between battalions.

*Masses, line of.*—A line of battalions in mass, with 10 paces interval between the battalions.

*Patrol.*—A body of men sent out to reconnoitre or to guard against surprise.

*Pivot flank.*—The flank on which a unit pivots when changing front.

*Pivot guide.*—A guide on the pivot flank of a unit.

*Position, change of.*—A movement by which a body of troops takes up a new alignment.

*Ranges, terms applied to.—*

| Terms applied to ranges. | Rifle. | Field Art. | Heavy Batteries. |
|---|---|---|---|
| | Yards. | Yards. | Yards. |
| Distant ... ... | 2,800 to 2,000 | 6,500 to 5,000 | 10,000 to 6,500 |
| Long ... ... | 2,000 to 1,400 | 5,000 to 4,000 | 6,500 to 5,000 |
| Effective ... ... | 1,400 to 600 | 4,000 to 2,500 | 5,000 to 2,500 |
| Close ... ... | 600 and under | 2,500 and under | 2,500 and under |

*Rank.*—A line of men, side by side.

*Squad.*—A small body of men formed for recruits' drill.

*Supernumeraries.*—The non-commissioned officers, &c., forming the third rank.

*Wheeling.*—A movement by which a body of troops brings forward a flank on a fixed or moving pivot.

## RULES FOR THE PRESERVATION OF HEALTH ON FIELD SERVICE.

### I.—THINGS THAT EVERY OFFICER AND MAN CAN DO TO PRESERVE HIS OWN HEALTH.

Remember that disease attacks you from outside: it is your business to keep it outside.

The following rules will help you to do so:—

*Water.*—Don't drink unboiled water if you can get boiled water.

Always start on the march and go on outpost or trench work with your water-bottle full. Cold weak tea (without milk or sugar) tends to assuage thirst.

Don't drink directly you feel thirsty; the oftener you drink the thirstier you will become. Drink as little as possible at a time, more especially if you are hot, and make up your mind to arrive at the end of a march with some water still left in your bottle.

*Conservancy.*—*Never* allow either urine or solid matter to remain exposed after they have been passed. The man who does or allows this is exposing his comrades to the greatest of all dangers on service—a greater danger than the fire of the enemy. Cover at once *with earth.* Remember that urine is just as dangerous as solid matter.

*Food.*—Never start on the march with an empty stomach if you can help it.

Never go on outpost or any detached duty without enough food to carry you over your probable time of absence, with a margin.

*Personal cleanliness.*—Remember that dirt is one of the commonest causes of disease. Dirt on your hands may mean poison in your food. Next in

## RULES FOR THE PRESERVATION OF HEALTH, &c.—*continued.*

importance come those parts of your body that are apt to chafe—as the inside of your thighs, private parts, &c. A bath is often an impossibility, but a wet cloth can do much to cleanse.

Remember that dirty clothes mean a dirty body; clean them as often as you can. If water is not available, crumple up the clothes, shake them well, and sun-dry them if possible.

*Vermin may be killed with petrol, hot ironing or scorching under-clothing.* It is comparatively simple, by attention to personal cleanliness, to destroy full-grown lice; but the eggs are killed with difficulty, for they are deposited in the seams of under-clothing, trousers, &c. Brush thoroughly, apply heat, or rub in the special grease (vermijelli), which smothers the young on emerging from the eggs. Dust also with vermin powder.

### II.—THINGS AN OFFICER CAN DO TO PRESERVE THE HEALTH OF HIS MEN.

*Water.*—On arrival in camp, or on taking up an outpost, see at once to the position of the water supply, and make arrangements for boiling. The collection of fuel for this purpose should be the first sanitary fatigue arranged for.

*Conservancy.*—Latrines and urinals should be fixed as soon as possible after arrival at a camp or outpost, and be placed where they cannot endanger kitchens or water supply.

Do not let your men ease themselves promiscuously.

Always leave your camp clean; others may have to occupy it after you, and they will suffer if you neglect this duty.

*Food.*—Remember that on service all disease is swallowed. See, therefore, that the cooking is carried out in as cleanly a manner as possible, and that food is protected from dirt both before and after cooking.

*Feet.*—Inspect the feet of your men regularly, and see that they do not neglect the smallest break in the skin.

*Personal cleanliness.*—See that your men get every opportunity of washing or dry-cleaning their clothes.

*Miscellaneous.*—Rest your men as much as possible. At halts, let them sit or lie down.

Always make them rig up some kind of shelter at night, for the head if for no other part of the body.

Watch your men, and see that every man that falls out often on the march, or any man noticed in camp going to the latrine oftener than usual, is made to report himself sick at once. The serious diseases of camp life all begin with diarrhœa, and this should, therefore, be looked on as a danger signal. It may mean nothing, but it should never be overlooked.

*Clothing* is intended to protect from heat, cold, and damp. See that your men use it accordingly. Warn them especially against neglecting to change wet clothes, when they can do so, and also against running the risk of chill to the stomach by not wearing a flannel or woollen belt.

## SALUTING OF OFFICERS.

Warrant Officers, Non-Commissioned Officers, and men will salute all Commissioned Officers whom they know to be such, whether dressed in uniform or not, including Officers of the Royal Navy, Royal Marines, Royal Indian Marine when in Uniform, Special Reserve of Officers, Militia, Honourable Artillery Company, Yeomanry, Volunteers and Territorial Force, and such Warrant Officers of the Royal Navy as have rank corresponding to that of the Commissioned Officers in the Army.

The salute, except when swords are worn, will always be with the hand further from the person saluted. When a Soldier passes an Officer he will salute on the third pace before reaching him, and will lower the hand on the third pace after passing him; when swords are worn the salute will be with the right hand.

A Soldier, if sitting when an Officer approaches, will rise, stand at attention, and salute; if a number of men are sitting or standing about, the senior Non-Commissioned Officer or oldest Soldier will call the whole to "Attention," and salute. When a Soldier addresses an Officer he will halt two paces from him and salute. He will also salute when withdrawing. When appearing before an Officer in a room, he will salute without removing his cap.

A Soldier without his cap, or who is carrying anything that prevents him from saluting properly, will, if standing still, come to attention as an Officer passes; if walking, he will turn his head slightly towards the Officer in passing him.

## NOTES ON FIELD COOKING.

*Hints for Preparing the Food.*

1. Keep yourself as clean as possible.

2. Keep the place tidy where the cooking is done.

3. See that the mess tin, or other vessel in which the food is to be cooked, is clean before using it. Directly after using the mess tin clean it on the outside and inside (if possible by boiling some clean water in it).

4. It is better to use clean wooden sticks than dirty crockery for handling and stirring the food.

*Firing.*

1. Do not chop the wood too small.

2. Do not use straw or similar things for lighting the fire.

3. Keep the fire burning evenly.

4. If wood is not available, dried camel's dung, peat, etc., make fairly efficient substitutes.

*Cooking.*

1. Do not leave the mess tin or other vessel empty on the fire.

2. Always keep water handy.

3. Stir with a wooden spoon or stick, and not with a metal spoon.

4. As a rule use the lid reversed and keep some water in it.

5. When using preserved vegetables they should be previously soaked in water; this may be done by using the lid of the mess tin when preparing the meals.

6. Dried peas or beans should be washed and soaked in cold water for twelve hours, if possible, before being cooked.

*Stewing.*

Stewing is the usual method of cooking meat, etc., under campaign conditions. The Soldier should understand that boiling is not stewing; rapid boiling makes meat tough, hard and stringy.

On the other hand stewing, *i.e.*, slow cooking just short of boiling heat, makes coarse meat tender and wholesome. Boiling meat, vegetables, etc., rapidly does not hasten the cooking, but spoils the food and injures the mess tin.

*Rules for Stewing.*

1. If sufficient water is available wash the meat and vegetables carefully before commencing to cook.

2. Cut the meat into pieces and cut up the vegetables (if any), and place them (with the bones if there is room) in the mess tin with sufficient water to just cover them.

3. Stew slowly for about 1½ to 2 hours, keeping the vessel closely covered. The length of time varies according to the size of the pieces and quality of the meat, but the cooking must be continued until the meat is tender.

If preserved meat is to be stewed, the vegetables should be first cooked till they are tender, then add the meat; let the whole stew gently for about ten minutes and then serve.

*Frying.*

Frying may be done in the lid of the mess tin, or a frying-pan may be made out of a preserved meat tin by melting the solder and flattening it out.

*Rules for Frying.*

When suet or dripping is not procurable, cut a little fat off the meat and place it in the lid of the mess tin. Melt the fat over the fire, and then place in the lid slices of meat, etc., and cook till done.

Plate VII.

*Fig.* 1.—COOKING IN THE FIELD.

*Fig.* 2.—OVEN BURROWED NEAR TOP OF A BANK.

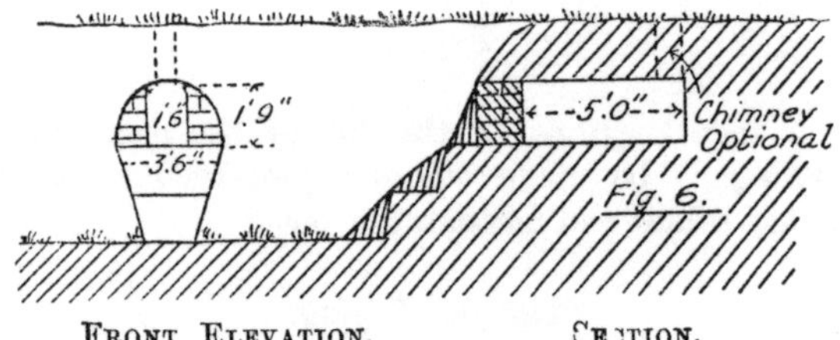


Front Elevation. Section.

*Fig.* 3.—KITCHENS.

Section of Cooking Trench.

Length varies with No. of Kettles, allowing 8 per 10 ft.

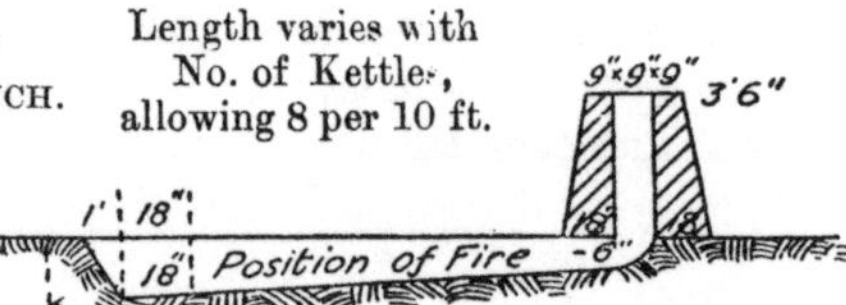


*Fig.* 5.

Raised Trench (wet weather).

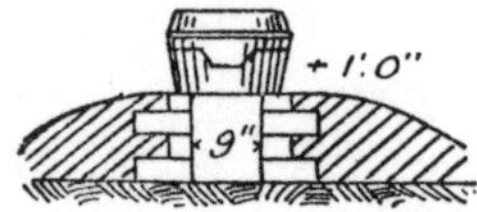


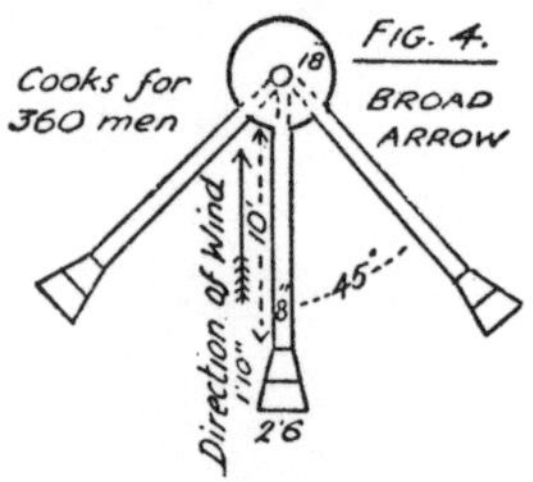


Kettles measure :—

12 quarts 9″ × 13½″ × 11″ high.
7 do. 8½″ × 12½″ × 8″ do.

*To follow Plate VI.*